iCONQUER

THE BLUEPRINT FOR TRANSITION
BLACK CHURCH/MULTI-ETHNIC CHURCH

DR. DERREN A. THOMPSON, SR.

ISBN: 978-1-7379939-0-2
ISBN (ebook): 978-1-7379939-1-9

Book design and formatting by Albatross Book Co.

For permission requests, please contact: hello@drderren.com

ACKNOWLEDGMENTS

I give honor and praise to God for His Holy Spirit that lives within me, leads me and has guided this entire process of writing this my first book, I Conquer.

Thank you to my beautiful wife of 24 years, Chalon Denise Melton-Thompson who has faithfully, sacrificially and courageously walked with me down every road that I have walked in ministry. Thank you for your prayers and for helping me walk by faith and not by sight. Your commitment to God is unshakable and I am better because of that commitment. Thank you for never giving up on me and for pushing me to stretch and go get what God has in store for me and for us! I love you deeply!

Thank you to the two heart beats outside of my body, Derren (DJ) and Darius. Thank you for the many days that you had to be the set-up team, the media workers, Sunday school teachers and my motivators all at the same time. Thank you for not getting offended when my time had to spent helping others. Love you guys deeply!

To my Mom who is an Elder at our church. Thank you for always making a way and for being my cheer leader even when you were the only one cheering. I will never forget all your sacrifices for me. You Rock Mother! Love you deeply!

To my wonderful church, The Conquerors Church in Edgewood, MD we have been through much together and we conquered it all. I am grateful for your commitment to serving God in our community. You made this work easy as we tested theory together. I am honored to serve as your Pastor!

And last, but not least, to Margaret Whibley my editor, thank you for making this book come to life!

I dedicate this work to three of my heroes, two have gone home to be with the Lord and never saw me finish this book and one still stands with me today. First to my Grandmother, the late Hattie N. Hill who was always one of my biggest supporters. She had a love for God that was inexpressible. Secondly to my Dad, the late Bernard M. Thompson, Sr. My Dad was my first member, first media director and chief supporter. Lastly, to my Mom, Rosa L. Thompson. My Mom has been my cheer leader and have supported me at every intersection of my life. Cheers to you Mother!!!

FOREWORD

I was once living the dream.

Beginning in 1984 and for eighteen years, I had been a student ministries pastor; and from 1993-2001, I served at a church that grew from 2,000 to 5,000 people. During those years, my youth group grew from 150 to 600 students and my paid staff from one administrative assistant to nine full-time people. Senior leadership provided the means for me to design, build. and pay cash to complete a $3.5M Student Center which included two stages, three basketball courts and a thirty-two foot climbing wall. In terms of salary, I was among the top two percent of paid youth pastors across the country. Literally hundreds of those students eventually served in short-term ministry and many to this day continue in full-time pastoral work.

Again, I was living the dream... until one day, in 1997, I looked around this otherwise amazing church and realized that the only people of color were janitors: and that began to bother me.

Over the next few years, I began to more closely examine the New Testament churches. Were these churches in fact segregated along Jewish and Gentile lines as I had been taught in seminary? While it may be pragmatic to plant, grow, and develop churches quickly by pitching the church toward a specific demographic, is such a practice biblical?

You might imagine what I concluded.

In 2001, then, I left that church to establish a church for all people in the urban center of Little Rock... a church whereby diverse men and women will themselves to walk, work, and worship God together as one to advance a credible Gospel in an increasingly diverse, painfully polarized, and cynical society... a church we called then and to this day, Mosaic.

For over twenty years, I have had the privilege of getting to know and coming alongside other disruptive innovators and ministry leaders who themselves are not afraid to challenge the status quo for the same reason. Today these men and women of faith, courage, and sacrifice, seek to establish and lead churches that extend faith, hope, and love to all people, not just some people. In so doing, they are addressing a fundamental question:

If the kingdom of God is not segregated, why on earth is the local church?

My good friend, Derren Thompson, is one such leader.

I had the privilege of getting to know Derren over the course of three years through a D.Min. program at Gordon-Conwell Theological Seminary led by Dr. Rod Cooper. Refreshingly, Derren was not in the program merely to earn a degree or title, and certainly not to fill his head with knowledge. From the beginning, his heart was engaged as we walked through the why, how, and what of developing a healthy multi-ethnic church. He was determined to apply biblical, educational, and practical knowledge in his own context. More than that, he articulated the need and expressed a passion to see other African American leaders embrace the vision of planting or transitioning healthy multi-ethnic churches, again, for the sake of the Gospel. Like the Men of Issachar who understood the times and knew what was right for Israel to do, Derren, too, understands the times in which we live. In ***I Conquer***, he provides a clear, concise, and compelling case for other African American pastoral leaders and churches to join him on the journey.

To be clear, building a healthy multi-ethnic church is not easy no matter the context in which we find ourselves. The past experiences, personal preferences, and personalities of those we seek to reach or lead for Christ via the local church seem ever to be in conflict with what Jesus otherwise expects of us, the local church, collectively, as He prayed on the night before He died:

> "...I pray also for those who will believe in me through their message, that all of them may be one, Father, just as you are in me and I am in you. May they also be (one) in us so that the world may believe that you have sent me... I in them and you in me—so that they may be brought to complete unity. Then the world will know that you sent me and have loved them even as you have loved me." (John 17:20-23)

Swimming upstream is never easy. Even so, there is no pass for degree of difficulty in the word of God; and Derren has embraced the challenge to do just that. Now, he's calling you, as well, to go where few in the past but growing numbers today are willing to go. Sure, there are obstacles ahead but we can overcome them if we act in faith and with intentionality to see a dream become reality.

As Derren writes, "To conquer means to overcome..." With this in mind, let me ask: what are you waiting for? Prayerfully, both Derren and I herein encourage you... Go forth and conquer!

DR. MARK DEYMAZ
Founding Pastor/Directional Leader,
Mosaic Church of Central Arkansas
Co-founder/President and CEO, Mosaix Global Network
Author, *Building a Healthy Multi-ethnic Church* and
The Coming Revolution in Church Economics

ENDORSEMENTS

"If you were to look up the word 'trailblazer' in Webster's dictionary you would find Dr. Derren Thompson's name next to the definition. Usually when a church wants to transition to a multi-ethnic congregation the change is from predominately white congregations to making the shift. Dr. Thompson is going into uncharted territory in taking a predominately Black church and transitioning to being multi-ethnic. The beauty of Dr. Thompson's book is that he not only shows you the city on the hill but charts a path on how to get there. Theory is theory until it becomes reality. Dr. Thompson's book is not theory--IT IS REALITY. If you're serious about reflecting the Kingdom of God on Earth and Pastor a Black church--this book is a must read. Dr. Thompson--MAY YOUR TRIBE INCREASE".

RODNEY COOPER, PH.D.
Former Kenneth and Jean Hansen Chair of Leadership and Discipleship at Gordon-Conwell Theological Seminary

In I Conquer Dr. Derren Thompson has taken the 21st Century Church back to its Multi Ethnic roots in the Acts of the Apostles. This excellent, encouraging, equipping, and empowering book will help Churches and communities bear 21st Century fruit for the healing of the nations. Thank you Dr. Thompson for this MUST-READ challenge for the traditional African American Church and all churches that love the Lord Jesus Christ!

BISHOP FRANK M. REID, III
Presiding Bishop, 11th Episcopal District
African Methodist Episcopal Church

Dr. Derren Thompson has shown great passion for seeing the church united across racial and ethnic lines. I am sure that his book "I Conquer" will help many in their transition to a more united church. May it be used for His glory!

DR. STEPHEN MAYO, LEAD PASTOR
Elm Street Community Church
Fitchburg, MA

Dr. Thompson I'm so excited for the work God is doing through you, and I anticipate the great impact "I Conquer" will have on progressing the church. As we both labored to complete our Doctorates, I not only heard your vision for the church, but prayed that God would move in a mighty way through your work. Congratulations on this major accomplishment, and as my grandmother would say, "God is not through with you yet". Keep climbing brother as I believe this book will be a tool used to move the church for years to come. Prayerfully!

DR. DERRICK BARKSDALE, SENIOR PASTOR
Duncan Creek Baptist Church
Clinton, S.C.

Every church has its challenges no matter the ethnicity of the ministry. But a church that is open to changing the face of its ministry is both progressive and forward thinking. As a black pastor who leads a multi-ethnic ministry, I commend Dr. Thompson's desire to see church beyond color. His approach to build a church that breaks the color barrier takes creativity, diligence, and a willingness to stay the course. Dr. Thompson understood the shift that was happening in his own ministry and knew it was going to require an adjustment in attitude, understanding cultural differences, and the steps necessary to bring healing and unity. If you are a pastor who has only experienced the black church but know you must move past the days of segregation in the church, this book is a must read. Congratulations Dr. Thompson for seeing through the lens of Jesus and not society.

R. KEVIN HOOKS, MTS
Lead Pastor, Life Nation Church

Dr. Derren Thompson's Mission, Message and Methods are DOPE! He knocks it out of the park with his approach. A Must read!

TREVOR J. CHIN, MAM
Executive Pastor/Co-Founder
Epiphany Church Baltimore

At a time for which the church is politically and racially divided, Dr. Derren Thompson's book, I Conquer, provides the keys required to unite the church. You will not be disappointed. Grace and Peace.

BISHOP MICHAEL T. SMITH, MBA
Senior Pastor
NBHOP

How fortunate we are in the body of Christ to have this man, pen this book, at this time. I am extremely proud of Dr. Derren A. Thompson, Sr for allowing God to lead him to writing I Conquer. This book really is a blueprint for transition. As his partner in marriage and in ministry, he lived this for several years!

Keep Going sir, Keep Going!!!

LADY CHALON M. THOMPSON, MHS
Leading Lady, The Conquerors Church
Edgewood, MD

CONTENTS

INTRODUCTION

Are you a conqueror? What does it really mean to be a conqueror, or to conquer? Do you have to be a powerful person? Do you have to be smart? Do you have to make a strong six or seven figures? Surely, you have to drive a Bentley, Beemer or a Benze to be a conqueror, right?

To conquer means to overcome and take control. When you decide to allow yourself to feel like you deserve to win even after feeling like you are always losing, you are a conqueror. When you decide that you will win with the hand that you have been dealt and no longer allow stumbling blocks to prevent you, you are a conqueror. When you decide that enough is enough, and that you will pick up where you are and take boldness off the shelf, and fearlessness off the shelf and place them in your personal bag, you are a conqueror. When you are able to look yourself in the mirror and declare that you kicked those things that hindered you in the teeth, you are a conqueror my friend. You have overcome, you have overthrown, and have subdued the earth realm, you are a conqueror and guess what, once you make the decision that you have conquered whatever has held you back, held you down, pushed you to the side as if you did not matter you will begin the process of conquering every situation.

I want to take you on a journey to conquer spiritually, emotionally, and physically. I will spend time sharing what has worked for me from a spiritual place, and I will share some of the emotional and physical strategies that have proven successful as I have journeyed with this work for the past twenty-five years. Are you ready? Let's go!

There are several bible verses that I will share that gave me the reasons for wanting to write this book. One of the Bible verses that arrested me when I read it was Isaiah 56:7b, where the prophet says, "For My house will be called a house of prayer for all the peoples." In line with this verse, Christians are charged with the task of creating a worship environment where every person from every culture should feel welcome. They should feel they have the spiritual tools to be successful. In 2017, I sought to create a method for doing precisely that. I took a local African American church plant and created the framework for a redemptive process that set the church on the path towards becoming inclusive and multi-ethnic. Specifically, More Than Conquerors Worship Center in Edgewood Maryland became a testing ground for a multi-ethnic church. The strategy involved surveys, questionnaires, teaching, and community outreach, and ultimately set in motion a transformative and redemptive process in which both the congregation and the surrounding community were involved.

This book tells the story of that process, and functions as something of a "how to" manual for other men and women who wish to transition their churches or ministry context from what it currently is to what it can become. It is a "how to" manual or guide for those pastors and church leaders who sense a need for and calling to diversify their congregations to the glory of God, and it will provide you with the tools needed to conquer in all area of your lives, regardless of your race, gender or age.

This whole transformative process was birthed from the African American church I planted and where I currently serve as pastor. Deeper study of the Scriptures convinced me that Christians are missing the mark in terms of what God has called the church to be. I decided to use the redemptive leadership model that has been taught (competency, principles, character, transformational, and redemptive) as my basis for moving the church from a place of being comfortable to a place that could be called the unknown, leaning on the power of God to direct and guide me in conjunction with my educational training. As I found through practical experience, redemptive approach to transitioning an African American church plant into a multi-ethnic context can help diversify the local church and community and even corporate America, thus altering the racial divide, if not in the world, at least one community at a time.

BACKGROUND

I grew up in the Catholic Church, where I had my first holy communion, was an altar boy and sang in the choir. It was an African American congregation with a white priest. That was my first introduction to diversity in the church. As I grew older, my family transferred our membership to the African Methodist Episcopal Church. There was little diversity there. We were taught about the black church, and sermons were passionately preached about black people and the struggle that black people went through to get where we were at that time. The founder of the African Methodist Episcopal Church (AME Church) was Richard Allen, and he started the AMEC because white Methodists would not allow him to use his ministry gifts. That movement pushed people to get in touch with their race and culture, but it also created a divide.

I left that church and moved to a non-denominational church that was also African American. That congregation was started from a church split from the AME Church but kept many of the same principles. It was at this church that I accepted my call to the ministry and became their youth pastor. I began to discern that there was more to ministry than just black people but decided that I would not openly share my thoughts as I was a part of a church where the pastor was the only one that was allowed to think, and if you dared try to think, you would be shut down. After staying in that context for many years, I received the call to pastor and plant a church in the suburbs of Harford County, Maryland. Our church was called More Than Conquerors Worship Center and God told me that he would bring people from all backgrounds to be a part of this church. We would not just be the average church; we would be different. I was not sure at that time what this meant, but I was clear that it would not be the norm. I had no desire to follow anything that resembled tradition and I was open to being different for God. I had to decide that different was acceptable. I spent the next five to six years waiting for God to send the masses and to send people that did not look like me so that we could begin to change the community and ultimately the world. As I waited, nothing happened. I began to study and learned of a doctoral program dealing with redemptive leadership in a multi-ethnic church context.

I knew that God was doing something in me, as I began to be invited to several churches that were non-African American to teach and preach. I would always ask why they didn't have diversity in their church. They would give me answers like, "This is a black church," or "I don't attract other races," or some would just say "Why do you ask?" It became clear to me that a stance needed to be taken, and as I prayed, I heard God say, *Why don't you lead the way*? I was being called to disrupt the norm in African American Churches. I was reminded of the words of Mark DeYmaz in his book *Disruption*, where he says, "Jesus Himself was a disrupter. In fact, you might say that He was and remains the disrupter of all disrupters"![1] From a theological perspective I gained a deeper understanding of the Word of God in Matthew 6:10, i.e., the portion of the Lord's prayer that states, "Thy Kingdom Come, thy will be done on earth as it is in heaven." It is the desire of Jesus that people from all walks of life and all races come together on earth as it is in heaven. I was also arrested when I read in Isaiah 56:6-7, that the desire of the Lord is that his house would be a house of prayer for all people, and that he wants to gather the people so that they come to him. That is God's purpose, but we are so divided. It is here that my journey began.

It is hoped that this book will have significant impact on the study and practice of redemptive leadership, especially in an African American congregation that is trying to transition. While a great deal of work has been done on general topics surrounding the multi-ethnic church and effective leadership development, I have not found anything on strategies for transitioning an already planted African American church to a multi-ethnic church. I have discovered several conferences on multi-ethnic churches, but they all seem to show the importance of multi-ethnic congregations, not how to make the transition. Additionally, there is little research on how to equip pastors to be

1 Mark Deymaz, *Disruption: Repurposing the Church To Redeem the Community* (Nashville, TN: Harper Collins, 2017), xx.

more open to this type of transition. The more that I speak with pastors across the country, the more I hear the same thing. They have questions on how to attract white members, and my white pastor friends struggle to find creative ways to invite blacks and Latinos to their churches. Many programs talk about diversity, and many grants are given to people to do diversity work, yet many churches are still segregated on Sunday morning.

For this reason, I have developed a model that I hope will extend the work that has already been done in this field by Mark DeYmaz, Derrick Anderson, and others, and enhance the resources available for those pastors and leaders looking for a new and creative way to do inclusive ministry. Additionally, it is hoped that this book will function as a one of its kind "how to" manuals that churches can use to develop and enhance their current ministry contexts.

WHERE IT ALL BEGAN: MORE THAN CONQUERORS WORSHIP CENTER

More Than Conquerors Worship Center was birthed out of a desire to please God and serve people who had been left out and pushed aside and those who find themselves trying to come up from behind. I started in ministry on May 31, 1996, and my desire at that time was to simply preach the gospel of Jesus Christ to the lost, lonely, and left out. I accepted my call to preach years earlier when I was growing up in the African Methodist Episcopal Church. Because of the political climate in that denomination, I sensed the leading of God to serve with my good friend at that time who was called to pastor a local community church in Baltimore. He asked me to come and help him, and I eagerly agreed. After preaching my first sermon, I was appointed as Minister for Youth and Young Adults. I was the youth pastor, in fact, and I was charged with building up that ministry area. I was given all the tools that I needed to be successful. This ministry grew so fast that I was promoted to a full-time position in the church as Minister of Administration. It was at that time that my pastor shared with me that this role would be short-term. I was supposed to be a sponge and learn as much as I could about the running of a church. He knew at that time that I was supposed to pastor and in retrospect, now that I think about it, I knew too.

After three years in that role, things became difficult in our relationship. We agreed that I would resign and start the process of finding a location to start More Than Conquerors Worship Center. The original plan was to start the ministry in a well-to-do and growing area in Baltimore County, MD, but my pastor changed that concept in the middle of the planning process. In short, relations became so strained that I resigned from the church the week before thanksgiving. It was unimaginably hard to sit at thanksgiving dinner without a job, bearing in mind I had just had a house built from the ground and was now unemployed. I had a wife and a five-year-old son, and my wife was pregnant with our second child. It was at that time that the Lord planted Romans 8:36-37 in my spirit. It reads as follows: As it is written, For thy sake we are killed all the day long; we are accounted as sheep for the slaughter. Nay, in all these things we are more than conquerors, through him that loved us" (Rom 8:36-37, KJV. I realized that I was in fact "pregnant" with More Than Conquerors Worship Center and did not even know it.

My former pastor made many promises concerning what he and the church were going to do to assist me in planting More Than Conquerors, none of which were ever fulfilled. I was scheduled to start the church in White Marsh, Maryland, but the pastor decided that I should move further out to a community called Edgewood.

The demographic and statistical profile of Edgewood, Maryland is as follows.[2] There is one high school, one middle school, and two elementary schools. As of the census of 2018, there were 262K people, the population density was 1,303.9 people per square mile (503.4/km²). The racial makeup of the CDP was 40.9 percent white, 43.7 percent African American, 0.40 percent Native American, 1.64 percent Asian, 0.09 percent Pacific Islander, 1.40 percent from other races, and 2.70 percent from two or more races. Hispanic or Latinos of any race made up 3.40 percent of the population.

There were 8,299 households out of which 43.9 percent had children under the age of eighteen living with them, 50.2 percent were married couples living

2 The statistics for the section that follows are taken from Wikipedia, "Edgewood, Maryland," https://en.wikipedia.org/ wiki/Edgewood, Maryland.

together, 19.3 percent had a female householder with no husband present, and 25.0 percent were non-families. Of all households, 19.6 percent were made up of individuals and 4.3 percent had someone living alone who was sixty-five years of age or older. The average household size was 2.81 and the average family size was 3.21.

In the CDP, the population was spread out with 32.2 percent under the age of eighteen, 9.0 percent from eighteen to twenty-four, 33.0 percent from twenty-five to forty-four, 19.6 percent from 45 to 64, and 6.3 percent who were sixty-five years of age or older. The median age was thirty-one years. For every hundred females there were 92.6 males. For every hundred females age eighteen and over, there were 87.5 males.

The median income for a household in the CDP was $63,497.

Crime in the area was at an all-time high and no one wanted to live in Edgewood, but my pastor wanted me to start a church there and be bi-vocational. I was determined that I was not going to fail, that I was a Conqueror and I wanted to surround myself with More Than Conquerors.

I asked the Lord how to get started and who I should ask to help me. I am a manager by trade, so organizing and leading is something that comes naturally to me. I started writing down what my vision was and how we were going to start this ministry. The Lord began showing me what to do and who to call.

I called a good friend who had been cashier for me when I managed a restaurant and shared with her that I was planting a church and that the Lord had told me that she was supposed to come and help me. Since she handled the money at the restaurant that I managed, she would manage the money at the church. God also directed me to call childhood friends. One was a vice-president of a bank and I asked him and his family to come along and help me. Two members from my old church also sensed a call from God to help me. So, I had my wife and my son DJ, along with Angie and Pat with their two children, and Duane and his wife, along with their two children. We had thirteen people including the children and we started the church with that group.

We started with Bible studies at the Edgewood Library for eight weeks before we began our worship services. We had flyers printed and canvassed the neighborhoods on Saturdays to connect with people and communicate that we were a new ministry with the aim of helping the community and its people through our teachings on how to "Live, Love and Learn." That became our church slogan and mission: showing people through the word of God how to "Live More, Love More and Learn More." The Bible studies went extremely well. People came each week and returned. While we were holding Bible studies, we were steadfast in looking for a building in which to hold our Sunday worship services.

As part of our planning, we wrote down all the things that made people not want to come to church.

We discussed the fact that people do not like coming to a long service, or a boring service, or a loud service. We thought about the people who did not like quiet services. We looked at whether people would want to be preached to loudly or taught. When we finished that session, we wondered if anyone would ever come as we had identified so many reasons why people would not.

We were a start-up church and had no money except for the tithe from the core team. We looked at buildings and were told repeatedly that if we did not have a certain amount of money, we could not use the space that we were looking at. We were told "no" so many times that we knew that our "yes" was out there. I prayed and asked God where I should look for a home for the church, and he told me to look at the elementary school. I called and asked if I could meet with the principal and she agreed. She told me that the building was available but that the process would be strenuous. After weeks of completing the forms and getting the needed insurance, we now had Sunday-only access to the school for a four-hour window. We decided on an order of service and started to promote the services. This was in 2005 when the world had not yet experienced the current social media boom. All our communications were through word of mouth, billboards, and print ads. We decided that we would start the church on the last Sunday in February.

Knowing what I now know about church planting, we made so many mistakes. We started the church in the winter, and we should have had better planning and marketing. Still, we used what we had, and God made us look so good. On our opening Sunday, we had about sixty people who attended the service and a few people joined the church. That was wonderful, but I was concerned about what the next Sunday would look like. Would we be there by ourselves or would God send us more people?

Thus, we began by having weekly Bible studies at the library and weekly services at the elementary school. Our growth was slow but impactful. We always had between twenty-five and fifty members at any given time. We were attracting people who did not have a prior relationship with Christ and so I spent the first few years teaching people the basics of church life. I had to teach them how to pray and to whom to pray. I had to teach and field questions about God and theology. It was a great start to my ministry. We were different in that we only stayed in church for ninety minutes and people would always say how different our church was. That is why we decided to use the theme "Come enjoy the difference." This slogan was attractive to many people and they started coming to More Than Conquerors because it was different. We welcomed everyone, but we did not make them stand up, put them on the spot, or hold a microphone up to their faces and ask for a testimony. We simply welcomed them. "If you like us, come back, but do me a favor and let me hug you before you leave today." We loved people and told them that we do not want anything from them; we want to give something to them. We started gaining respect because we were approachable, and we showed up when people were hurting or when people needed help. We would show up at funerals; we would show up when someone was having surgery; we would show up to the school for tutoring; and at the football fields to show our support. We were different in the eyes of people in the community, but we were just doing what we knew to do. We wanted to love the people.

The people.... Edgewood is a great place, but when you are from beyond the Edgewood community, especially the Edgewood church community, you are treated like an outsider. I have been in this community for twelve years and people still treat me as if I am an outsider. I am from Baltimore City and they want to know why I am starting a church here. In fact, one lady told me to go back where I came from, that I was not wanted or needed in this community. I realized later that people are afraid of what they do not understand. The people wanted a fresh and new ministry, but they had trouble trusting pastors. I had my work cut out for me. I wanted to win the hearts of the community and so I had to be where the people were. I started appearing at the Boys and Girls' Club. I started buying pizza for the teachers at the school, and they started letting me speak in their classrooms. I started an after-school program for boys and then set up times to meet their parents. I went to school board meetings and county council meetings. I met the elected officials and told them what I was trying to do and asked for their help. We started winning in the community. People started coming to More Than Conquerors to see what we were about. I found that the people in this community wanted a real experience with church and that we only had one chance. We had one chance to make a difference or else we would not be given another opportunity. I found poverty at a new level in this community. The average income in this community was $40,000 per year, but in many instances, that was for families of four or five people, which is poverty. There is low-income housing and while the official crime rate was fairly low, Edgewood had serious issues with gangs. Everyone was concerned about the gangs and how they affected their children. People were scared to leave their houses and they were scared to allow their children (mainly the boys) to go outside to play because of the gang activity.

Edgewood is a factory town. Most of the families have one or two family members working at a factory. The main factories in this area are Kohl's, Rite Aid, Macys, and Clorox Bleach. These employers moved their businesses to Edgewood to help deal with poverty by providing jobs. They offer rotating schedules and rotating shifts. This has worked well for people to get to church because they could meet us for what we called "The Church at Study" on Wednesday evening at 7 p.m. and "The Church at Worship" on Sunday mornings. We started telling everyone that if they came to our services it would be the most productive ninety minutes of their week. We toyed with the idea of having daytime mid-week Bible study, but that did not work well in our context.

We found that people in this community liked

going to the mall and attending children's sporting events. Football and lacrosse were events that this community really rallied around. They would show up in large numbers to see the children play recreational sports. The great things about the sports events were that we could host a few of these events in our building. This was important because people began to trust us as a church, and we stood on our integrity. We worked hard at doing what we said that we were going to do. We started living by the principle that we would always keep our word.

At this point in our journey, we were an African American church. Local pastor and noted author David Anderson shared with me that if you want peaches, then you need to plant peaches. You cannot expect to harvest something you have not planted. I planned a black church because I did not know any better. Out of the sixty-nine churches in Edgewood, there is only one church where the membership is multi-ethnic, but that is not reflected in the leadership of the church. Thus, the racial makeup of our church was all black.

I wanted the church to look like a church that Jesus would pastor. This meant taking what we were noted for in the community to the next level. In 2012, I started going into different communities to develop relationships. I started teaching our congregation that God's desire for each of us is to be inclusive, and we started diversifying every area of our church. I asked white people what they would like to see in church, and what types of worship spoke best to them. I asked my Hispanic friends what was most important to them in a worship service. I found that we were more alike than different. I found that black people as well as white people want the message to be clear and understandable; they want to be in a warm and friendly place; and music was important to both as well. With intentional effort, More Than Conquerors started to become a multi-ethnic church.

When we started More Than Conquerors, we wanted to be known as the church that cares, the church that helps, and the church that teaches the Word of God in a warm and passionate way. Now fifteen years later, we have hundreds of partners, because as a result of the pandemic, our ministry has gone global. Our initial thirteen members are still with us and all are working as leaders in the ministry. We have partners that are a part of every generation as well as gender. We have black, white and Hispanic members as well. Most of our membership work professional jobs where they make between $60,000 to $110,000 per year. I do not have any members who have learned of the work that we are doing and then moved to the community. However, we do have many members who were in the community and have come to call More Than Conquerors their church home. They have grown in their walk with God. They have learned faith and how to exercise their faith. Many of them have experienced serious trials and heartbreaks. Many have experienced setbacks, health issues, and in some cases mental breakdowns; but they are still determined to walk by faith. In short, they have decided to be conquerors. Many of them shared with me that they came to this church defeated and devastated, but that they have learned to conquer. It has encouraged me to see them walk by faith in every area of their lives. We are a church that that is called upon as a subject matter expert of community connecting from a faith-based perspective. The existing members are at the point now where they are helping me teach the newer members how to live a life of faith and believe God for the greater things. It has been amazing watching some of the men in our church learn how to pray, and then teach their families to pray.

More Than Conquerors has grown in its ministry to men, women, and young people. We have an outreach team and a help ministry. We are about community outreach, but we spend a great deal of time on internal ministry as well. Our congregation wanted to become a multi-ethnic church. We wanted to be a welcoming church to all people, not just black people. And so we started working towards that goal. What we found was that people were searching for a sense of belonging. People wanted to feel they belonged to someone or something. Our team thought that if we could work hard and move out of our comfort zone, we could really have a significant impact in this community.

As an example, one day as I was driving through the community, I saw a lady pulled over to the side of the road. She was standing beside her car looking troubled and uncertain. I pulled over and asked if she was okay, and she shared that she had run out of gas, did not have any money, and could not get anyone on the phone to help her. I went to the gas station and found someone with a gas can. After we put the three dollars' worth of gas in her car and got it started, I asked her to follow me to the gas station so that I could fill it up for her. She was amazed at the gesture, and it dawned on me that she was not the only one in need of gas. I immediately met with my team and my assistant Angie and we were able to pull together a free gas give-a-way in the community. We realized that black people, as well as white, Asian and Hispanic people have something in common: we all need gas for our cars. We partnered with our local Chick Fil-A owner, Michael McFerran, who offered free sandwich gift cards for everyone. The gas station where we held the event also partnered with us and gave away free slush drinks to everyone. It was a great day and we were doing ministry for the community at the same time. We met the needs of over a hundred people that day with gas, beverages and sandwiches: a win-win for the community.

The community has changed a great deal. When we started, we had twenty thousand people in the city, with an average salary of $56,000 per year. There are new homes being built and the communities are starting to live work and play together. When we arrived, we were treated as outsiders and we decided that we would work to ensure that other pastors that came to this area would not have to experience the coldness that we experienced. We wanted to develop camaraderie with other pastors, so we established a ministerial alliance that would allow clergy to meet monthly to do things that require the help and assistance of all of us. We now have a joint Thanksgiving worship service, as well as a "Back to Church" joint marketing campaign where we each put the name of our church on a flyer and invite people to come to any of our churches. We also share together in the Global Day of Prayer celebration each year. These opportunities help us to come out of our local church and be a part of the greater church: we call it the Church of Edgewood.

This community has changed because the people are starting to have a mind to work. They are excited about the changes in the community, and they feel they are a part of something great. That makes living in this community much easier. In our communication with local pastors, we work together to meet the needs of the people that we serve. We have sponsored spaghetti dinners, clothing giveaways, as well as gas giveaways. The community did not look this way fifteen years ago. The county has taken an interest in Edgewood and has made tremendous structural enhancements. We have a new high school and two new middle schools. The structures that were in place were torn down and new schools were built. Additional businesses have come to the area, bringing new jobs to the community.

One thing that was missing in our community was a church that is multi-ethnic. Many pastors that I work with have either all-white churches or all-black churches. Many talk about wanting a diverse church, but none of our congregations seemed to be moving in that direction. I mentioned earlier that we had one ministry in our community that claimed to be multi-ethnic, but the pastor refused to meet with the other pastors. While that is sad it is not surprising. Many people will hold a good multi-ethnic conversation, but it remains just that, a conversation where nothing happens. Thus, it became my desire to spend the following years changing that mindset in my ministry context. I wanted people from all backgrounds, all races, and all ethnicities to feel free to worship together, bowl together, cook food on the grill and share a hotdog together, but most of all to learn from each other while collectively learning more about God.

I shared my vision about the need for us to become multi-ethnic in our ministry context, and the concept was well received. I started connecting our ministry with different alliances that would help us break into the demographic to which we are called. I conducted meetings with my team and we connected nationally with several multi-ethnic ministries. I exposed our congregation to the mindset that we are better together. My pastor colleagues thought that I was crazy and a few said to me that I needed to stop this multi-ethnic stuff before I turned my members away. But I am thankful to God that he chose me to follow this process. It is sad that as pastors we do not all feel the same way about people. It amazes me, but I did not let that stop me.

I have had to make changes along the way that have helped my ministry. I have relaxed my dress by not wearing suits or robes. I no longer preach in a celebratory style for the entire message. I have transitioned my style more to teaching. I still celebrate; I just don't shout until I am out of breath. I have started to see that our efforts are working. We have begun the process of transitioning the church and have several white families that are now a permanent part of our church. They enjoy the church and have become great supporters and willing workers. We are still working on the Hispanic population. The good news from our fellowship sessions with our guests is that Hispanics would like to see a Hispanic on the staff, and even an interpreter, and we are looking for an Hispanic leader to join our team.

In 2019, my brother Pastor Trevor Chin from Epiphany Church, Baltimore, sat with me to help me rebrand our church. We changed everything about our service, our marketing, our brand. We started doing things that we had never done as a church and our team was on fire. Pastor Trev designed a new logo that spoke to who we were, and he rebranded our internal and external marketing so that we would become a cutting-edge ministry. We purchased new lights, media equipment, a podium, flags, banners, and welcome cards. We even set up a coffee station and allowed people to take their coffee into church. This was new to me because I grew up in a traditional church where you were not supposed to even chew gum, let alone drink coffee. The change had to start with me. Our consultant, Pastor Trev, helped us move from to antiquity to modernity. We put flags outside that flew so high people started recognizing that something different was taking place at our church. In an effort to simplify things, we even changed the name of the church. We had been More Than Conquerors Worship Center; however, now we were the Conquerors' Church. What we found was that keeping the membership looped in and allowing them to feel as if they were a part of the changes made all the difference in the world.

However, shortly after our ministry refresh, we came up against Covid-19. Still, what the enemy means for evil, God has a way of turning around for good. We had to move to holding 100 percent of our activities online. We thought that we were ready; however we learned that there is a difference between being ready and being excellent. I am a Pastor who believes in excellence, and so we worked hard to find our way to excellence. We started on Facebook Live, and then realized that anything can go wrong with live feeds, and so we started pre-recording and uploading our services to YouTube. We asked our members to join us on YouTube, and our friends and visitors to join us on Facebook and Twitter/Periscope. We held our Bible studies on Facebook Live and our small groups on Zoom. We started having a weekly check in immediately after our Sunday service, and we called it "Happy Hour." It was a time to ensure that our members had enough PPE and food as well as cleaning supplies. We held food giveaways and support groups for members who contracted Covid. We now have daily prayer calls each morning at 6am and we have watched and are watching God do great things.

We are making a difference one family at a time and our church-wide slogan has not changed in fifteen years. We are still the church that teaches people how to Love More, Live More and Learn More, and for that I am grateful.

STEP 1:
THE STAGE OF PREPARATION

INTRODUCTION

When we make a decision that we want something different, there is always a process that we must follow. There are steps that need to be taken in a very systematic way to ensure that we are meeting our goals. While I will talk about things that needed to change in my church, I want to be very clear that whatever the process of change you are working through, there will always be forces that will stand in your way.

Have there been some issues or strongholds that have stood in your way? Have there been issues that have made you take a second look at yourself? If we are honest with ourselves, we have all been there. Why not take the bold step today to admit that there have been things that have held you back from being the person you know God called you to be? Will you take the bold step of admitting that there have been people you have allowed to hold you back from being all that God has called you to be?

It starts with a decision. When you are sick and tired of being sick and tired you will get to the intersection of the Already, but Not Yet. I had to get to a place of understanding that life teaches each of us lessons and that a lesson not learned will always be repeated. That's a hard pill to swallow, but it is a true statement. I have allowed people in both the church and the corporate arena to have more power over me than they deserved. Things got a lot better when I decided that I held the keys. You hold the keys to your destiny. Ask God to take you to that place where you are no longer worried or concerned about the opinions of people. You matter, yes, you count. Get this: get rid of the people in your circle who do not understand your worth. They do not matter! God has the final say.

In this next section I talk about starting the process that God has told us to start.

WHEN GOD SAYS, "MOVE," HE IS HOLDING THE TRAFFIC BACK TO ALLOW YOU TO START CROSSING INTO YOUR NEXT DESTINY. THIS WILL NOT MAKE EVERYONE HAPPY.

I had to learn that there are some people assigned to our lives just to be a distraction. Name your distraction.... Is your distraction called Lissa, or Andre or Marcel? Is your distraction a relationship or even your career? Name your distraction, so that you can call it out before God.

The first step in transitioning to a multi-ethnic church takes place with the existing congregation, and the need to lay a foundation through preaching and teaching that clearly conveys the biblical message, what God wants in this matter. For a transition in thinking needs to take place, as well as a physical transition, in the way we as the body of Christ view church, and the work of the church. In what follows,

I provide some examples of the Bible's teaching that ministers can use to inspire and gather the support of their congregations. For of course, such a transition cannot take place without the full support of the congregation.

When reading the Bible and paying careful attention to the ministry of Jesus, we should be able to walk away with a clear understanding of God's plan for the Kingdom of God and the church. The plan of God is that His people come together as one body to worship Him. The biblical and theological justification for transitioning any church into to a multi-ethnic church can be found throughout Scripture. Throughout the Bible, in both Old and New Testament passages, it is made very clear that multi-ethnic ministry is the will of God. God never desired that we should have segregated churches. His intention was not to have a black church or a white church, but instead a church that looks like the Kingdom of God. He wants a church that will not only see color and value it but will also see his awe-inspiring framework and understand the true gift of an inclusive culture. From the very beginning, there have been references to God's plan for multi-ethnic ministry. I have selected a few examples from Scripture that aimed at assisting anyone seeking to engage in such a multi-ethnic ministry. I am aware that not everyone will agree with this type of interpretation, nor will all agree with the inferences that I will draw. However, the discussion can spark a dialogue about bringing us closer together, instead of drawing us apart and serve as a starting point for others. As a pastor interested in effecting change, you may choose different passages. For my part, I selected passages in Scripture that arrested me when I read them. In the process I became very intentional about my viewpoint and a little more open to other viewpoints.

THE GOSPEL OF MATTHEW

In Matthew 6:9-10, Jesus is recorded as saying: "In this manner, therefore pray: 'Our Father in heaven, Hallowed be Your name. Your kingdom come. Your will be done On earth as it is in heaven.'"[3] What was Jesus talking about when he said, "On earth as it is in heaven"? This was Jesus' initial teaching, when he was teaching the disciples what is known as the Kingdom Prayer. This prayer is not only found in Matthew 6; there is also a version in Luke 11:2-4. It is more than just a prayer, however; it is Jesus teaching the disciples to seek God's coming Kingdom. In other words, He is teaching the disciples to pray for what is to come. The prayer has several different features that need to be explored before addressing the key points of the passage. It begins with "Father," or "Our Father." This is important, as it denotes a level of authority that immediately requires an attitude of reverence. Craig Keener writes: "We must understand what God's 'Fatherhood' would have meant to most of Jesus' hearers."[4] For in first-century Jewish Palestine, children were powerless social dependents, and fathers were viewed as strong providers and examples

3 Bible references are from the NKJ Version, unless otherwise stated.
4 Craig S. Keener, Matthew, *The IVP New Testament Commentary Series* (Downers Grove, IL: InterVarsity, 1997), 141.

on whom their children could depend. Jesus summons us to pray, not like the pagans (6:7), but with a dependence on God as our Father (6:8-9), who watches over us. This is very important, because we can understand that in many ministry contexts, especially the black church context, children have issues with trust. They are not easily persuaded to trust anyone enough to call them "Father." I know this to be true as I have served in many pastoral contexts where fathers have disappeared, and children left fatherless. These children have experienced broken promises; they have experienced abandonment; and in many cases, they feel powerless to provide for themselves. Bringing them into the context of the church and teaching them how to pray to "Our Father," is something that is foreign to them. Jesus teaches that this is how we should respond to the Father as the prayer begins. This opening denotes dialogue and encourages us to see God as one who will never walk out on us, as one who will always be there for us no matter what. This prayer thus starts off in a way that draws the reader in.

The second portion of the prayer describes reverence. We recognize that we are praying to God the Father, and now we are introduced to the fact that he is to be reverenced and that our focus should be on Him and His glory and not on ourselves. The fact that He is a holy God who desires our reverence, and in fact requires it, is awe-inspiring. God's name should be hallowed. This term "hallowed" derives from the Greek word *hagiazō,* which means to render or acknowledge, or to venerate or hallow.[5] The word helps us to understand the posture we need to adopt when coming to God in prayer. The fact that this requirement to "hallow" is part of the prayer indicates how order is established at the very beginning. As believers, we long for the coming of God's Kingdom, and are aware of the wonderful opportunity that we have to do/complete His will. Keener describes this as anticipation of the time when there will be no more crime, no more discrimination, and no more hatred, sickness or grief.[6] Hallowing God's name also means observing His will, so that His will and favor are not delayed in the life of the believer. Keener notes that while many believe that the Lord's prayer is an end time prayer, but has implications for here and now. George Ladd writes that, "Modern scholarship is quite unanimous in the opinion that the Kingdom of God was the central message of Jesus."[7] Ladd discusses the Kingdom of God as described by Matthew: "He went about all Galilee, teaching in their synagogues and preaching the gospel of the kingdom" (Matt 4:23). This thought about the Kingdom of God encourages us that the Kingdom of God is almost here but not yet. Ladd notes that many scholars, such as Albert Schweitzer, Johannes Weiss, and C.H. Dodd have reached a consensus "that the Kingdom is in some real sense both present and future."[8] The concept of the Kingdom of God has a rich history of bringing people to Christ and allowing humanity to

---

5 Blue Letter Bible, blueletterbible.com, s.v. "hagiazo."

6 Craig S. Keener, *Matthew*, The IVP New Testament Commentary Series (Downers Grove, IL: InterVarsity, 1997), 141.

7 George E. Ladd, *A Theology Of The New Testament* (Grand Rapids, MI: Eerdmans, 1974), 57.

8 Ladd, *A Theology Of The New Testament*, 59.

learn the things of God and experience the richness of the Kingdom. It also allows for a very deep promise that as we live in and experience the Kingdom of God, what we have seen is not all that God has for us. Ladd writes, "The expectation of the coming of the eschatological Kingdom in Jesus' teaching was nothing new."[9] He continues, " C.H. Dodd is right in affirming that the most characteristic and distinctive of the gospel sayings are those which speak of a present coming of the Kingdom."[10] This allows for the continuous push to work in the Kingdom of God and enjoy the benefits of the Kingdom of God. This becomes part of our daily work as we continue to push to win people to Christ in the Kingdom of God.

The next segment of the prayer arrested me: "Your kingdom come. Your will be done On earth as it is in heaven." When I began this whole process, these words arrested me, because it became very clear to me that I had misunderstood the will of God. I had been driven by tradition and not necessarily by the word of God. "Thy Kingdom come, thy will be done," pushed me to ask, "What is His will? Is it His will that black people come together every week and worship the same savior as white people, yet not do so together?" After reading this Scripture and after consulting numerous commentaries, the realization of what God's will is began to sink in.[11] David Guzik writes

9 Ladd, *A Theology Of The New Testament*, 65.

10 Ladd, *A Theology Of The New Testament*, 65.

11 Craig S. Keener, *Matthew*, The IVP New Testament Commentary Series (Downers Grove, IL: InterVarsity, 1997), 141-143; Craig S. Keener, *A Commentary on the Gospel Of Matthew* (Grand Rapids, MI: Eerdmans, 1999), 218-219; Frederick D. Bruner, Matthew, *A Commentary: The Christbook* (Grand Rapids, MI:Eerdmans, 2004), 303;Craig L. Blomberg, Matthew, The New American Commentary (Nashville, TN: Broadman Press, 1992), 118.

in his commentary that the will of God should be such that people will align themselves together to reach a common goal.[12] The call of God has always been that men and women of all races should come together to be the people of God, working together in the Kingdom of God. Guzik comments that everyone wants to guard their own name and their own reputation, but that we must resist the tendency to protect and promote ourselves first, and instead put God's name, Kingdom and will first. We need to understand that this prayer is focused on the community as a whole, and not just one area of the community. It is the desire of Jesus that the will of God be done on earth the same way it is done in heaven. In heaven there is no concept of race, there is no hurt, and there is no destruction. There is no disobedience and there are no obstacles to God's will. On earth there are many obstacles to God's will, and in many instances people (and even believers) do not understand that the will of God is important and will ensure that the church is a place of peace and worship, a place where everyone is welcome regardless of race or gender. Guzik writes in his commentary on Matthew in the *Blue Letter Bible* that one should understand that the citizens of Jesus' Kingdom will want to see His will done as freely on earth as it is in heaven.[13] In fact, he who taught us this prayer used the very same prayer himself. When he was in the Garden of Gethsemane he did not dispute the decree of the Father, but simply cried, "Nevertheless,

12 David Guzick, "Study Guide for Matthew 6," *Blue Letter Bible*, www.blueletterbible.com https://www.blueletterbible.org/Comm/archives/guzik_david/studyguide_mat/mat_6.cfm

13 Guzick, "Study Guide for Matthew 6."

not as I will, but as thou will" (Matt 26:39). While he was on the cross and the bloody sweat was pouring down his face, when all the fear and trembling of a man in anguish were upon him, he did not dispute the decree of the Father, but bowed his head, said "It is finished," and yielded up his spirit (Matt 27:50). These few verses in the Gospel of Matthew exemplify the position of Jesus and why it is that he wills transformation in the church. Another careful look at the position of Jesus as reflected in the Kingdom Prayer of Matthew 6 is offered by B.C. Caffin, who writes about the words "In earth as it is in heaven," as follows:

> There the holy angels ever do the blessed will of God; they do it perfectly, they do it cheerfully, without self-denial, without painful effort. There is no place in heaven for a will that is opposed to the will of God. The presence of such a will would be a contradiction to the everlasting harmony, a note of discord in the angelic song. It is not so here. Our wills are distorted by inherited corruption, by our own consent to sin.[14]

This comment further emphasizes the point that the will of God is important for the "now" time. Not only does this particular commentary suggest that we must approach the will of God in order to do it, it implies that it will be a difficult task. It is very clear that as Christians, we look to do the will of God, but in many instances, we do not know the will of God.

14 B. C.Caffin, *Matthew*, The Pulpit Commentary, vol. 15 (Peabody, MA: Hendrickson, 1985), 243.

Many Christians believe that after their Wednesday Bible study and their Sunday service they have done their Christian work until the following week. That is far from the truth: our job as Christians is to see the will of God and to make carrying out that will a priority. It should be a priority for the church to look outside of its walls to simply see what is there. When doing this, the church must ask the question, does our church look like the community that we serve? If the answer is yes it does, the church then needs to see how it can move to the next level of Christian work. If the church is situated in an all-white community or an all-black community, or in an all-Asian community, and the answer to our question is yes, we are in an all-black or white community and our church consists of all whites or all blacks, we nevertheless have the option to do more and try and bring different people into the church so that the church is more in keeping with God's will. If the answer to the question is no, our church does not look like the wider community, then we have an obligation to start bringing people in who may not look like us, talk like us, or even smell like us. That is when we begin to do the will of God. This is what our appetite as Christians should feel like. We should feel uneasy just accepting the status quo. We know that Jesus had a plan and that the plan was to do and teach the will of God. He taught this as a part of the Kingdom Prayer. Jesus recognized that it is very hard to pray this prayer when trouble is heavy in our lives. When we are afflicted with pain and sickness, when those that we love are taken from us, it is hard to pray this prayer. Jesus knows that it is hard and he never told us that it would be easy. He did say that he would be with us every step of the way, however. Thus when speaking of transformation and changing things, we are reminded that Jesus showed us that he himself was willing not to take the easy route. As Caffin notes in his commentary, if a holy angel were set here on earth in our position and in our surroundings, that angel would operate in the same way that we should, seeking to do the will of God. This is our high calling; nothing short of this ought to satisfy us, and this is in fact what we pray for daily. We should always be striving to live as each new day comes, more nearly as we pray. While engaging with this Matthean form of prayer, there is a pattern according to R.T. France. He notes that in this powerful prayer there are three segments that call for our attention. "There is an opening address which is our father in heaven. Next there are three clauses about God and His worship: May your name be held in reverence; May your kingdom come; may your will be done, as in heaven so also on the earth." He also points out that there are three petitions for our own needs: "Give us today the bread we need for tomorrow. And forgive us our debts as we, too, have forgiven our debtors. And do not bring us into testing, but rescue us from the Evil One."[15] This framework of the Kingdom Prayer, and in particular the verse, "Your will be done," establishes an important premise for transforming churches into ones that more closely reflect the composition of our

15 R.T. France, *The Gospel of Matthew* (Grand Rapids, MI: Eerdmanns, 2007), 242.

communities, and thus become more like the Kingdom of God.

In summary, Matthew's gospel shows us that we are a part of the Kingdom of God, and being a part of this Kingdom comes with a great responsibility. It is an inclusive responsibility to win souls for Christ and to be at the forefront of leading change. This Kingdom prayer has elements from the past, but also allows for a great future. The "right now" seems bright. Matthew helps us to see a tremendous relationship that we have with God, and shows us how to seek the Glory of God first and not our own, and lastly helps us to understand that this is not our struggle, but the Lord's work. The passage shows us that we have to have total dependence on God.[16]

ISAIAH 56:7

As I continued my journey to discover biblical passages to support my theory that the transformation of an African American church into one that is multi-ethnic is the will of God, I alighted upon the Old Testament Book of Isaiah, in which there is a recurring theme. Isaiah 56:7 is another very subtle example of God pushing people to follow His will, along with the acknowledgement that the will of God is not something that we automatically fulfill. We need to do something concrete in order to fulfill it. In Isaiah 56:7, God is recorded as saying: "Even them I will bring to My holy mountain. And make them joyful in my house of prayer. Their burnt offerings and their sacrifices will

16 Keener, *A Commentary on the Gospel of Matthew*, 216-220.

be accepted on My altar; For My house shall be called a house of prayer for all people."

G. Rawlinson writes in the *Pulpit Commentary*, "The temple or house of God stands for his kingdom of righteousness; and in exalted vision the prophet foresees the time when it shall stand open to every man—to the stranger or heathen and even to those physically debarred. It is to be called 'a house of prayer for all people.'"[17] The word house here comes from the Hebrew word *bayith*, which translated means "home" or "house containing a family." This word helps us to understand the sense of inclusiveness that pervades this passage. God's house of prayer is intended for all people as a safe haven for humanity to come and share, love and be loved. It is a place for families that is open to all people. The word "all" means complete or entire, which helps us get a better understanding of who God is speaking about through the prophetic voice of Isaiah. It is also here that the temple is designated for strangers as well as Jews. It is designated for people from everywhere to have a meeting place where things can happen. This is a place where miracles can happen. It is a place where people come because they love God and want to keep his commandments. It is thought that if you love God, you will serve Him, and to serve Him means that you will keep His commandments. This is not only a place of prayer, but a place of sacrifice as well. John Oswalt notes that the prophet was inviting foreigners to be a part as an act of inclusion. This inclusion would be

17 G. Rawlinson et al., *Isaiah*, The Pulpit Commentary, vol. 10 (Peabody, MA: Hendrickson).

for those foreigners who "keep justice and do righteousness."[18] He comments that there are benefits that God offers to the foreigners, such as bringing them to his holy mountain. God will meet them there and will spend time with them there and will treat them as he would any other believing Israelite.

Matthew Henry writes in his commentary in the *Blue Letter Bible* that in this place (the house of prayer for all people) one can count on three things happening:

Firstly, there will be assistance in this place. People can come here and find what they are looking for. This is a place where you can expect that your needs will be met, regardless of what they are, and in many cases be met to overflowing.

Secondly, there will be acceptance in this place. There will be no need to worry about people liking you or treating you oddly. You will not have to worry about being accepted as an Asian or an African American. Acceptance is in this place, for all people, for the entire people to be welcome to come and to share, be fed and to experience the true love of God. Lastly, Henry notes that this is a place of comfort. It is a place where one can find the comfort needed to be able to rest well in Him.[19]

Oswalt notes that the foreigners welcomed by the Llord are characterized by three behaviors. "They

18 John N. Oswalt, *The Book of Isaiah* (Grand Rapids, MI :Eerdmanns, 1998), 459.

19 Matthew Henry, "Commentary on Isaiah 56,"*Blue Letter Bible*, 12-15-2017 https://www.blueletterbible.org/ Comm/mhc/Isa/Isa_056.cfm?a=735007

have joined themselves to the Lord. They have joined themselves to God in order to minister to him, to love his name and to become his servants. The most immediate observation that one can make concerning these is that none of them speaks of joining oneself to the Lord for the benefits of that relationship. The joining is out of a desire to benefit the Lord."[20]

At More Than Conquerors we put it like this, "You can come as you are, but you won't leave as you are." In other words, transformation will take place. The church that Henry and Oswalt describes sounds like the type of church I wanted to be a part of: a church without spot or wrinkle, a place where people can cast all their cares and burdens on God himself. People become one in such a place, sorrow becomes joy in such a place. It is a place where those with problems come and receive possibilities. It is a place that is reserved for all of us.

JOHN 17:1-5

John 17 contains another passage that I would like to look into more deeply. In John 17:1-5, Jesus defines his mission and its scope. He declares that he has been given authority over all humankind and to all those the Father has given him he will in turn give eternal life. He calls all of us to "know" Him, not just some of us:

> Jesus spoke these words, lifted up His eyes to heaven, and said, "Father, the hour has come. Glorify Your Son, that Your Son may

20 Oswalt, *The Book of Isaiah*, 459.

> glorify You, as You have given Him authority over all flesh, that He should give eternal life to as many as You have given Him. And this is eternal life, that they may know You, the only true God, and Jesus Christ whom You have sent. I have glorified You on earth. I have finished the work which You have given Me to do. And now, O Father, glorify Me together with Yourself, with the glory which I had with you before the world was." John 17:1-5

For centuries, this particular passage was a prayer widely referred to in theological circles as the "high priestly prayer" of Christ. The prayer gives credence to those who have been charged with simply proclaiming that we have a right to eternal life. It is important to understand the timing of this particular prayer. It takes place the night before Jesus will die on the cross. In terms of the setting, Jesus has already had the last supper with the twelve persons who are supposed to be his supporters, and he has already washed their feet. He has reinterpreted the Passover, and has identified Judas as his betrayer. We can thus imagine it as a trying and emotional time for all those assembled. This provides the focus for why this prayer is even uttered at this time. The prayer can be broken into three parts:

First, Jesus prays to his father for himself: "The hour has come. Glorify your Son, that your son may glorify you, as You have given Him authority over all flesh, that He should give eternal life to as many as You have given Him" (John 17:1-2). This is where Jesus lays out his mission and states his purpose. In *Building a Healthy Multi-Ethnic Church,* Mark DeYmaz writes:

> The term rendered "know" is a translation of the common Greek word, *ginosko*, meaning simply, "to know." To know in the full sense of this term, however, means to learn or acquire knowledge through experience. In other words, Christ does not so much pray that these will come to know God intellectually (the term, *oida*, in the Greek) but rather that they will come to know God more fully in and through their own personal experience. In order to know God experientially, we must come to know His son, by faith, that is, Jesus Christ who has been "sent" by the Father. The term sent is a translation of the Greek word *apostello* which translated means, "one who has been sent as another's personal and authoritative representative."[21]

What this means is that Jesus is very clear about His mission, which is to proclaim the message of eternal life to all humankind. His desire is that all humankind come to know the love of His Father, embrace Him by faith and receive the most precious gift of all, eternal life. That is His desire when he starts praying.

Second, in the next section of the prayer, Jesus turns the attention from himself and places it on the disciples. He is very clear that he will no longer walk with them, talk with them or assign them tasks, so he

---

21 Mark DeYmaz, *Building a Healthy Multi-Ethnic Church* (San Francisco: Jossey-Bass, 2007), 6

goes to the Father to ask Him to "keep them in Thy name so that they might be one." He wants them (and us) to experience the joy of the Father:

> That they all may be one; as thou, Father, art in me, and I in thee, that they also may be one in us: that the world may believe that thou hast sent me. And the glory which thou gavest me I have given them; that they may be one, even as we are one: I in them, and thou in me, that they may be perfected in unity; and that the world may know that thou didst send me, and didst loved them, as thou didst loved me.

Thirdly, there is final section of the prayer, which bears on those who will likewise embrace the message and the mission of Christ. In other words, Jesus is praying for us, for all those who desire to be one with God. He is praying for oneness throughout this prayer. I appreciate the intention of the text, since Jesus prays one thing three times in three verses, and that is simply that we will become one.

Biblical scholarship teaches that whenever something in the text is repeated often, it is repeated for a purpose. The overwhelming theme of oneness continues to ring out loudly as we dig deeper into this passage. Christ prays first that we will "be one" (John 17:21), then a second time that we may be seen to "be one" (John 17:22) and, finally, that we would be "perfected in unity" (John 17:23).[22] This is a message to all

22 DeYmaz, *Building a Healthy Multi-Ethnic Church,*8.

those who come after the disciples and who embrace Christ by faith and subsequently receive eternal life. This message is for anyone and for all. There are no stipulations concerning race, gender, creed or demographics. It is for all people. Additionally, the word "perfected" is translated from the Greek word *teteleiomenoi,* which in this context means "to become mature or, completely one." In other words, Christ prays for one thing in this prayer, as stated, but it becomes increasingly clear and emphatic. Christ is praying that future generations of believers will be one so that humanity will know that the call of God is that we should all come together as one and be partakers of the love of Christ as one functional unit, and not be separated. Christ states that His mission will be accomplished by other people for the very simple purpose of God being glorified. While this might not be an easy task, it is certainly biblical, and as Christians our desire should be to do the will of God for the right reasons at all times. I believe this is what Paul means when he writes in Ephesians 4:1 that we should walk worthy of the calling with which we were called. This passage is significant, because it should in its simplest form mean that when we all come together for the sake of the gospel, we are coming together to please and glorify God. All of God's children, from diverse backgrounds and with differing biographies, should connect and share the things that make us similar, instead of focusing on the things that tear us apart. Then we can be confident that we are experiencing life on earth as it is in heaven. Our job in the local church must be to adopt the mission of Christ, which is to see humanity saved, and work together for a common cause. When this type of unity in the Spirit takes place, it becomes what Stephen Covey writes about in his book, *The Seven Habits of Highly Effective People:* it is a "Win-Win."[23] Everyone involved wins, and most of all, the Kingdom of God wins. God receives the glory and He allows us to live in the experience of what it is like to live on earth as it is heaven. I shared with my church that God is so gracious that he gives us many wonderful gifts. One of these gifts is the gift of choice. I shared with them that when I get to heaven, I do not want them to take me to my room only to find I have many unopened gifts waiting for me, and ask the question, "Why do I have so many gifts in my room?" I do not want to hear the response, "I had all these gifts for you on earth, but you would not open them. I was trying to give you heaven while you were on earth, but you would not receive it."

I want all of my gifts now and so I exercise my gift of choice and I choose to make God my choice and allow Him to promote me, simply because I am doing His will. This has to do with a desire to simply do His will.

GALATIANS 3

A further passage that I found useful in building the biblical foundation for the transition to a multi-ethnic church was Galatians 3, with an emphasis on verse 28. Paul starts this letter by recognizing that

23 Stephen Covey, *The Seven Habits of Highly Effective People* (NY: Free Press, 1989).

the Galatians have launched their Christian experience by faith, but now they are seemingly content to leave their journey of faith and chart a new course based on works, which is a direction that Paul is having problems with. His letter seeks to get the Galatian Christians to understand that works will not sustain them; it is their faith that will sustain them. Paul launches a defense of faith in this letter. He begins by being very clear about who he is and sets the tone by setting out his credentials as an apostle and saying that he has a message from God for them. He wants them to know that blessings come from God based on faith and their ability to walk by faith, and not by the Law. He informs them that the Law is designed to determine a person's guilt and imprison them when guilty, but that faith sets them free and allows them to enjoy liberty in Christ. He stresses that to have liberty is to have freedom, and that freedom in Christ means to produce the fruits of righteousness through a spirit-led lifestyle. It is important to note that this is the only one of Paul's letters where there is more than one church. In Galatians 1:2 it is written, "and to all the brethren who are with me. To the churches of Galatia." In 3:28 Paul helps us to understand the importance of breaking down silos and embracing diversity and inclusion: "For you are all sons of God through faith in Christ Jesus. For as many of you as were baptized into Christ have put on Christ. There is neither Jew nor Greek, there is neither slave nor free, there is neither male nor female; for you are all one in Christ Jesus" (Gal. 3:26-28).

Paul begins to draw the conclusions that follow

from his lengthy discussion of the promise to Abraham. The main focus here is on the word "all." This is an inclusive word that is translated from the Greek *pantes*, which means each, the whole or everyone. Paul is therefore saying that all Galatian believers, without distinction, are already children of God in Christ Jesus by faith. In 3:28, Paul breaks down three simple points that allow us to understand fully the point about inclusiveness in the church today. It is suggested in the NIB commentary that Paul is probably quoting an early Christian baptismal formula, and if so he is calling to mind the words that have been pronounced over each of the Galatian believers at the time of baptism, words that declare unmistakably the obsolescence of the Jewish/Greek boundary that the missionaries are trying to reestablish through their advocacy of circumcision. The radical vision set forth in this formula reflects the new creation that God has brought into being. The three binary oppositions that characterize all human existence in the previous age have been dissolved. I will examine each of these oppositions in turn.

Firstly, there is no longer Jew or Greek: This is the element of the formula that Paul particularly wants to emphasize in the present context. In the old era, the Law protected the religious and cultural separateness of the Jewish people, setting them apart from all other peoples (collectively categorized as "the nations.") In Christ, however, the separateness is abolished, because Jews and Gentiles are constituted together as one new people of God. Considering this new reality, ethnic distinctions no longer matter. The implication of this is, of course, that circumcision as a marker separating Jews from Gentiles no longer matters.

There is no longer slave or free: Distinctions of social class are negated in the new creation. The identity of Christians as "children of God" is given to them by their participation in Christ; consequently, they are now related to one another as brothers and sisters and are no longer in a social hierarchy that distinguishes slave and free. The baptismal formula declares that social class and power have been delegitimized in Christ. Admittedly, the already/not yet tension in Paul's thought leaves room for uncertainty about the extent to which this eschatological vision of equality is to be embodied in social practice. The key to understanding Paul's thought on this question is to recognize that he sees the church as an alternative community that prefigures the new creation in the midst of a world that continues to resist God's justice. Thus Paul is not calling for a revolution, in which slaves rise up and demand freedom; rather, in this verse he is declaring that God has created a new community, the church, in which the baptized already share equality.[24]

Thirdly, there is no longer male or female: Paul makes no use of this opposition in the argument of Galatians, one piece of evidence that suggests that he is quoting a formula. Attentive readers of the NRSV will note that this third element breaks the formal

---

24 J. Paul Sampley, *2 Corinthians, Galatians, Ephesians, Philippians, Colossians, 1 & 2 Thessalonians, 1 & 2 Timothy, Titus, Philemon,* Vol. 11 of The New Interpreter's Bible (Nashville TN: Abingdon Press, 2000), 272.

pattern of the previous oppositions: there is no longer a or b; there is no longer c or d; there is no longer male or female. Paul is echoing the language of Genesis 1:27: "Male and female he created them." To say that this created distinction is no longer in force is to declare that the new creation has come upon us, a new creation in which gender roles no longer pertain. The fact that the letter to the Galatians is not concerned with gender roles does not diminish the force or importance of this element of Paul's vision for the church as a transformed community. If the church is to be a sign and foretaste of the new creation, it must be a community in which gender distinctions—like the ethnic and social distinctions noted in the first two parts of the formula—have lost their power to divide and oppress. This does not mean that those who are in Christ cease to be men and women any more than male members of the community cease to be circumcised or uncircumcised. Rather it means that these distinctions are no longer the determinative identity markers, no longer a ground for status or exclusion.[25]

The implications of Paul's extraordinary baptismal declaration of the new creation are summed up in the final clause of vs 28: "For you are all one in Christ Jesus." The summation of this passage looks to the need to be one unit that functions for a single purpose, and that is to glorify God and share with each other the goodness of God in an inclusive manner. It signals the need to offer a worship opportunity that encourages everyone to come and share and fellowship

25 Sampley, *2 Corinthians, Galatians,*etc., 273.

around the Word of God. This unified worship does not look at race, gender or socioeconomic status, or whose house is the biggest, but allows everyone to share their gifting for the betterment of the community. This is what God would want, and so this is my pursuit.

REVELATION 7: THE FOUNDATION FOR INCLUSIVENESS

In Revelation 7, John writes about inclusiveness in ways that I had not been aware of prior to setting out on this path. The setting of Revelation 7 seems to shift from what is happening on earth and moves to what will happen in heaven, specifically, what will happen in the heavenly throne room as described in Revelation 4 and 5. Here in chapter 7, John records a vision. Scholars call this a proleptic vision, which is the representation or assumption of a future act or development as if it were presently existing or already accomplished. John has a vision of the redeemed of the Lord in heaven, not now, but in the future, when God's plan has been accomplished and the redeemed people of God stand united as one. It is a vision of inclusiveness. The text reads as follows: "After these things I looked, and behold, a great multitude which no one could number, of all nations, tribes, peoples, and tongues, standing before the throne and before the Lamb, clothed with white robes, with palm branches in their hands" (Rev. 7:9).

"After these things, I looked" (7:9) indicates that a new vision is being introduced. This time, instead of seeing 144,000 people from the tribes of Israel, John sees "a great multitude that no one could count, from every nation, from all tribes and peoples and languages." This vision is a fulfillment of the Abrahamic promise in Genesis, in which God tells Abraham that he will become a great nation and through him "all the families of the earth shall be blessed" (12:2-3). Abraham's offspring will eventually become as numerous as the stars in the sky, the dust of the ground, and the sand on the seashore (Gen 13:16; 15:5; 22:17; 26:4; 28:14). In the spiritual descendants of faithful Abraham, that promise is now fulfilled, for they constitute a throng that is beyond counting. This innumerable crowd is inclusive, encompassing people from every racial, ethnic, political, and linguistic background.[26] This text makes it clear that it is the will of God to include all people in the work of ministry and in the work of God. In other words, we see in this text that there is a joyous celebration, as John does not envision a small gathering of a select few. It is not closed to a single group or racial class. It is not open only to black people or to white people. It is a joyful celebration of worship where everyone from every race or class is welcomed and encouraged to participate. It is a redemptive group of people who are happy to come together. I believe that there are democrats, republicans and independents at the celebration. I am sure that there are fat people as well as thin people; there are smart people and some that experience challenges, but everyone has a place. In this text, we see

26 Mitchell G. Reddish, "Revelation," *Smyth &Helwys Bible Commentary* (Macon, GA: Smyth and Helwys, 2001)147-148.

that God has thrown a party and the place is overflowing. John's vision is of a God who welcomes a massive crowd of faithful servants, reminiscent of Jesus' joy-filled parables of the lost coin, the lost sheep and the lost son (Luke 15).[27]

Looked at this way, the text is very clear, and I would argue that this is an inclusive, welcoming, festive celebration, where God is pleased that the people of God have come together as one. We can find a few simple details that support this theory:

- The great crowd is not just anywhere: they are around the throne of God. This is known as the reigning center of God; it is oneness with him in His very presence.
- The people are clothed in white robes, which is the color of victory, the color of celebration and purity.
- They have palm branches in their hands, which indicates the festive nature of this gathering, for palm branches are a symbol of celebration and victory.

While it is important that we can envision this type of interaction in heaven, as believers in the Lord Jesus Christ, we have to start the process of allowing ourselves to live with these principles now on earth "as it is in heaven." We recognize that we are all placed here on earth for a reason. Paul writes in Ephesians 4 that we are all on earth for a reason and each for/with a different calling. We are all called to something and it is incumbent on each of us that we

27 Reddish, "Revelation," 149

work toward that calling. Inclusiveness is the will of God. The New Testament church is designed to draw people closer to God. In *The Community of the King*, Howard Snyder writes, "I am impressed that the early Christians and the New Testament writers understood the church as part of God's dramatic, historic action in Jesus Christ of reconciling all things to himself,' things in heaven and on earth' (Eph 1:10). The bible calls this reconciling work the kingdom of God."[28] In several different places in scripture, God reveals that His desire is that through Jesus Christ all will come to know Him. He reveals that His desire is that people will come together and work together and worship together, so that His Kingdom might be glorified. Snyder writes that God has a master plan not only for us, but for His Kingdom. We know that a master plan is a clear blueprint of the finished work. We use a blueprint to work out how to get to the end of a project. The blueprint helps us to start, move, progress, bring in additional supplies and shows us where to go, when to go, and how long to stay. The blueprint is the compass, the GPS; it is the master plan. Snyder writes, "But what is God's master plan? Simply this: that God may glorify himself by uniting all things in Christ. God's plan is to unite and reconcile all things in Christ so that men [and women] can again serve their maker. The bible version is of all earth's peoples, and in fact all creation, unified in praising and serving God (Ps 67:3-5; Rev 7:9-12; 19:6)."[29] As I read through the New Testament, God's plan is revealed. Paul writes about God's plan in

28 Howard A. Snyder, *The Community of the King* (Downers Grove, IL: Inter Varsity Press, 2004), 10.
29 Snyder, *The Community of the King*, 65.

many of his letters, but the one letter where this concept of inclusion is clearest is Ephesians, and especially 1:10:"[T]hat in the dispensation of the fullness of the times He might gather together in one all things in Christ, both which are in heaven and which are on earth—in Him."

It is here that Paul reminds us, as he has reminded us in several other places, that it is the will of God that we be inclusive. We see inclusion in the worship in Revelation 5 as well. When the people of God come together to do the work of ministry, God gets the glory and we live out our divine purpose in Him. It is wonderful to see how the New Testament call of God can be found in so many different areas of our ministry:

It can be found in our worship—when we all come together as one and worship, lift up our voices collectively in a display of worship, it is a sound that is so tremendous it is a drawing in to the Holy of Holies.

The call of God can be found in our witness—at time of writing, I was in the Knotts Library in Baltimore at St. Mary's Seminary. This is primarily a catholic institution, where seminarians are studying to be priests. While writing, and going back and forth to fetch different books and commentaries, I met Scott, a second-year seminarian who wanted to be a priest. He introduced himself and it was clear that he had a love of God. He said that he saw me pull up in my car and wanted to know what type of car it was. I said that it was a Lexus and he said "wow." I wanted to know why he had asked and he said that as priests and seminarians, they live very simple lives. I said that my theology was a little different; that I believe that it is the will of God that I live a blessed life; and that the God that I serve would not withhold any good thing from me. He asked me to share more and I began to witness to Him about how I see Jesus and how I lead the church where I serve as pastor. After fifteen minutes of sharing, Scott said, "Thank you for your witness." This incident showed me that people are watching us, and if I had responded in a way that made Scott feel his views were unimportant, or that I was too busy to talk with him, it would have diminished my witness. Our witness through inclusion is so vitally important. In many cases we only get one chance to make a great impression of God in the lives of people. Scott already knew Christ, but for all those persons we come in contact with that might not know Him, our witness is so important.

The call of God can be seen in our evangelism. When we stand in our differences as brothers and sisters, and as one unified body showing the love of Christ, it is infectious.

The call of God is in our outreach—when we seek to serve the lost, lonely and left out and do it in an inclusive way, we are saying to the community at large that we are one. We are saying that the issues that we have faced and in some instances, are facing now, will not define us. We will show the world, one community at a time, that He is faithful to His word and that He will honor us as we reach across the lines of division and show the warmth of inclusion and the warmth of embrace, which is ultimately showing the love of Christ, on earth as it is in heaven.

CONCLUSION

Jesus teaches us that it is the will of God for all of us to walk together to show the love of Christ to all human beings. We have many opportunities to show this love in various ways. One of the ways is to decide once and for all that doing so is in fact the will of God. Once we are able to reconcile this in our minds and in our hearts, the work begins. The work will come very easily if we open ourselves to reach across the aisles to help and encourage each other and do the work here on earth, as it is in heaven.

The passages I have discussed in this chapter are just some of the examples from Scripture that pastors can draw on as they prepare their congregations for opening up to multi-ethnic ministries. While the theology in this chapter goes pretty deep, and it is fine for those who want to pastor or are already pastoring, what does this mean for those who are reading this because they truly want to know how to begin to live a life that conquers? It is clear that it is the will of God for us to partner together, work together and worship together. What can you do to grow yourself and move from a place of devastation to a place of divine destiny? You can follow these steps:

- Make a decision today to go for what you want
- Find an accountability partner you will listen to

- Engage in an information gathering season
- Find trusted individuals who agree with you about your dreams
- Find someone who is already doing what you want to do
    - o Ask if you can meet with them for fifteen minutes to pick their brain
    - o Find out what they did, how they did it, and who else they recommend you connect with.
- Sow a seed to show God that you mean business
- Start doing what you have planned to do: Understand that you will make mistakes along they way, but understand that God will give you more on your way than He does when you first get started
- Take faith steps, some measured and some not measured
- Assess where you are and keep going while making adjustments
- Trust God for the next steps in the vision.

STEP 2: LEARNING FROM THE EXPERTS

I have been fortunate enough to pastor a great church. I am also a college professor; a business owner; a recruitment, diversity, equity, and inclusion professional; a counselor; and a coach. I am also a husband, father, and friend to many. Despite all that, I still need people. There are many things that I have not yet learned and still need to learn. That is the reason I will always be a student. I enjoy the art of learning, and so am always asking questions and learning from those who know more than me. I have formal as well as informal mentors I can call in every avenue of my life. One thing that I have found as I have tried to lead people, is that people are afraid of asking for help. We don't know what we don't know...

And so want to push you into another dimension. In this new dimension, begin to push yourself to ask for help: help in understanding, help with a project, help growing, help getting your attitude together, and even help trying to figure how to invest. We all need help and in this next section I want to share with you how I was able to learn from the best.

Most of the material that follows comes from engaging with authors from related fields who offer insight on transitioning a church, and by looking at their processes, and learning from them. I use works by Mark DeYmaz, whose books have helped me to birth this vision. Other authors that I draw on include Efrem Smith, David Anderson and Brent Zuercher, and David A. Anderson. I also explore the work of key authors on the subject of basic church planting and multi-ethnic transitions.

Many churches have been planted for this age and time; however not many churches planted in one style are now trying to transform their current ministry model and turn it into something different. With most church plant designs, the church is established and simply grows from that point, maintaining the same kind of focus. The research resources on transitioning a church, and making it in to something different from when it was birthed, are sparse. The purpose of this chapter is thus to identify sources that can to contribute to the process of transitioning an African

American church into a multi-ethnic church. Much of the available literature does not directly address the matter of making a black church into a multi-ethnic church, although in many instances it does discuss the transition process in general. Topics discussed widely in the literature include leading a transition, working through a transition, responding to a transition, as well as the theology of transition. While many resources are available to assist church planters, the majority discuss how to get black people to come to a white church. There is little or nothing available for black churches that seek to invite white, Asian, native Americans and Hispanic parishioners. In fact, outside of Gordon Conwell Theological Seminary, I have not found anyone addressing this topic, and the concept of Redemptive Leadership in the black community is more-or-less unheard of.

Michael O. Emerson and Christian Smith have now opened the door to a critical conversation about race relations, however.[30] Importantly, they show how divided Christians are in the context of their faith. For many years there has been a need to not only look at, but to ask questions about the racial divide is central in our cultural context. Emerson and Smith open the door for us to consider where we have been, what is happening now, and to suggest ways that we can move forward. As Christians, we are still trying to figure out how to continue to do God's work in the midst of a pandemic. We are trying to figure out what to say so

30 Christian Smith and Michael O. Emerson, *Divided by Faith: Evangelical Religion and the Problem of Race in America* (Oxford University Press, 2001).

that every hearer can walk away with something that will make them feel good. Race relations are at an all-time low in the country right now. I have appreciated the calls and texts and emails from my white Pastor friends and just friends from other races as well. My good friend, Pastor Brook, who pastors a local congregation near our church, reached out to me as we were preparing for a rally in the community right after the George Floyd murder. He said, "Derren, you and I are friends and I will not pretend to understand what you are going through, but I would love to have a conversation just so that I can learn and grow through this." I so appreciated that call and Brook and his family stood with me and my family as we walked and held a peaceful protest in our community. It did not stop there; we continued to talk and challenge each other about what we would say to our congregations.

In the corporate arena, it was frustrating to hear people say, "Don't all lives matter?" This was negating what African American people are feeling and continue to feel while living in this society. I shared that as the father of two black sons, I am concerned when they leave the house and it should not be like this. I appreciated Brook because he said, "I don't know, so help me." Others that I work with in corporate America tried to fake their way through, working hard not to say the wrong thing, even though what they were saying was in fact the wrong thing. While we all know that diversity, equity and inclusion is all-important, I would submit that games are still being played. Evil and divisiveness are still at the top from a priority perspective.

We are seeing things right out in the open that we had never seen before, although they were still happening. They were just behind closed doors. Those in leadership still have the arduous task of trying to plan the next move towards equality for everyone. We are still believing the day will come when we can all just get along. We do not have to always agree with each other's perspectives, but we should be able to get along. At the time of writing, a sitting state representative from Georgia was arrested for simply knocking on the door of the governor's office, while he was signing a bill that would no longer allow voter freedom. We continue to see the rough and the wrong; however we will still speak power and a new day.

With this door into renewed race relations now open, we have the charge to boldly walk through, remembering to be careful not to close our eyes and ears to the unpleasant things that we may see or hear as we journey. Thus, we should embrace the very thing that makes us uncomfortable in the race relations process. I suggest that as we walk, it is important to be fully equipped to do so and not be afraid to enter areas that might be a little difficult. Emerson and Smith are not afraid of different experiences and for proffering opinions boldly. It seems that we often shy away from conversations that could bring about change in our lives and in the life of the church. The key focus or thesis of Emerson and Smith's book becomes clear in the first couple of chapters. They want to expose the state of race relations in the church. They look at the role, or what they interpret as being the role, of white evangelicalism in black-white relations. While this is a worthy topic, it is my opinion they should have done additional research to balance the books. There may have been some pioneers in the field of race relations that have been left out.

The term "racialized" describes the process of imposing a racial interpretation on people and texts, and their analysis suggests that we still have problems with how we deal with race. They are correct; race is still a problem. Even with many kinds of churches, it is still a problem; even with a former African American president, it is still a problem; and even in the wake of 9-11, instead of us all coming together, we are still very much divided.

THE CHURCH IS DIVIDED. AND IN THE UNITED STATES, THE CHURCH HAS BEEN DIVIDED FROM THE DAYS OF SLAVERY.

Floyd Massey and Samuel McKinney point out:

> The religious life of slaves was severely restricted by their masters, even though some were less oppressive than others. Officially, a

> white person had to be present if they were to meet as a body for worship. Hence, the early black church became an invisible institution which met secretly. Such unlawful gatherings of black people were the beginning of the black church. They had to meet at times that would be safe from the dusk-to-dawn scrutiny of the patrols of the slave owners.[31]

Considering this history, and with a clear understanding of how black people have been treated as part of that history, it is a difficult task to look beyond what has happened and press towards a better future. Moreover, many people who are Bible readers do not understand the need for this type of work or study. Many have asked why I am dealing with this issue. Why not allow the black church to be the black church and the white church to be the white church? Others seek to share with me the history behind the racial divide in the black church, stemming from the time when black minister, Richard Allen, was not allowed to lead worship in the Methodist church. After many occurrences of not being allowed to use his gifts, he and many others left the Methodist church and started the African Methodist Episcopal church.

The church has come a long way since then, but nevertheless still has a long way to go. For this reason, I begin with an analysis of the materials that I have found to be most relevant to my chosen path of

---

31 Floyd Massey, Jr and Samuel Berry McKinney, *Church Administration in the Black Perspective* (Valley Forge, PA: Judson Press, 1976), 13.

creating a multi-ethnic church, and I also expand on perspectives from authors working in various related areas of ministry. This chapter is not intended as an exhaustive exploration of all the literature, but it will offer points that allow for discussion. I draw insights from authors who speak of the need for transitioning a church, regardless of where that church is now. It is simply a matter of getting the church to a place of diversity where everyone can feel welcome.

BUILDING A HEALTHY MULTI-ETHNIC CHURCH

One cannot have a dialogue about the multi-ethnic church without reference to the fathers of the movement. One such individual is Mark DeYmaz, whose second book is one of the foundational works on the subject.[32] It is a book that takes us on a biblical journey, as well as the secular journey of how DeYmaz came to plant a diverse church in a community where race has always been an issue. Little Rock, Arkansas, is a place where racial issues became a national story, for it was there that the Little Rock nine were the first black students to enter a white school. This important event that took place in 1957, but the racial atmosphere of the 1950s was still prevalent in 2001 when DeYmaz and his wife Linda made the tough decision to stay in Little Rock and plant a multi-ethnic church. There was nothing like it in the area. DeYmaz surveyed people from the inner city, as well as those in the suburbs. He spoke with business owners and even those catching buses, because he wanted to

32 Mark DeYmaz, *Building A Healthy Multi-Ethnic Church: Mandate, Commitments, and Practices of A Diverse Congregation* (San Francisco, CA: Jossey-Bass, 2007).

make sure there was a need for a church that welcomed people from all walks of life. DeYmaz knew that there was a call of God on his life to reach beyond the racial divide and create something that had never been created before, and so he planted Mosaic, a congregation which became a known as the "church for others," the church "for all people." The vision statement for the church reads: "Mosaic is a multi-ethnic and economically diverse church founded by men and women seeking to know God and to make Him known through the pursuit of unity, in accordance with the prayer of Jesus Christ (John 17:20-23) and patterned after the New Testament church at Antioch (Acts 11:19; 13:1ff.)."[33] With the power that comes from this mission statement, DeYmaz laid the foundation for building a multi-ethnic church. It is important to note that DeYmaz started building this church from a perspective that embraced diversity.

David Anderson spoke at the 2016 Mosaic Conference in Dallas, TX, and said that if you want apples, then you will need to plant an apple tree; likewise, if you want oranges you will need to plant an orange tree. That made a great deal of sense, but what do you do if you plant an apple tree and decide later that you want not just apples, but fruit in general: oranges and pears and watermelons? DeYmaz outlines what to do in principle, arguing the biblical foundation will work for every context. He establishes the theology for the multi-ethnic church, taking the reader through three different passages in Scripture that help frame this undertaking. This I view as the strength of his work.

33 DeYmaz, *Building A Healthy Multi-Ethnic Church,* xxvi.

He shows us the prayer of Christ, the pattern of the New Testament Church, and what he calls "the Pauline Mystery," as expressed in the Book of Ephesians.

The prayer that DeYmaz speaks about, which forms the theology for the multi-ethnic church is found in John 17:1-5:

> Jesus spoke these words, lifted up His eyes to heaven, and said: "Father, the hour has come. Glorify Your Son, that Your Son also may glorify You, as You have given Him authority over all flesh, that He should give eternal life to as many as You have given Him. And this is eternal life, that they may know You, the only true God, and Jesus Christ whom You have sent. I have glorified You on the earth. I have finished the work which You have given Me to do. And now, O Father, glorify Me together with Yourself, with the glory which I had with You before the world was.[34]

After Jesus prays for himself, he immediately begins to define his mission and his scope. Jesus is given "authority over all mankind" and to those the Father has given Him, He will, in turn, give eternal life.[35] In the second part of the prayer, Jesus turns His attention away from Himself and focuses on "them" to whom He has been sent. He prays that the Father will keep them as one. He already knows that he will not be with them, and so is praying that the Father will give them the ability to stay connected and not

34 Unless otherwise stated, all Scripture references are from the NKJV.
35 DeYmaz, *Building A Healthy Multi-Ethnic Church,* 6.

fall behind. In Philippians 2:2, Paul later expresses this as being "of the same mind." Jesus wants His disciples to retain the same spirit and the same love for one another that they currently have. This is important to Him. He also asks God to keep them from evil. He knows that not everyone will welcome the unity that they will share and that not everyone will understand the word of God, and so He wants the Father to keep them or shield them from that. He also asks the Father to sanctify them in truth. In John 17:18, He articulates the actual task: "As thou didst send Me into the world, I also have sent them into the world." What we see here is that in this second section of this great prayer: 1) Jesus offers a prayer for himself stating that he is sent from God to declare the salvation message to men and women that they might believe; and 2) He commissions the disciples to carry on the mission and He asserts that if the Father keeps them in "thy Name" and they stay "one," this will be a successful journey.

The impressive thing as we continue to read the Scripture, is that we see that they did exactly what was required of them and completed the task. DeYmaz writes that the last part of this great prayer in John 17:20-26, concerning oneness of mind, love, spirit and purpose, is equally vital for all those coming after the disciples—those who will likewise embrace the message and the mission: "I do not ask or pray on behalf of these alone, but for those who also believe in Me through their word: (John 17:20).[36]

DeYmaz thinks that the New Testament pattern of inclusion leads us in a particular direction. In Matthew

36 DeYmaz, *Building A Healthy Multi-Ethnic Church,* 7.

28:19, Jesus is clear that he wants the disciples to "go." He wants them to go and make disciples of all the nations. Yet DeYmaz points out that we must read the book of Acts almost to the end before we find anyone willing to leave Jerusalem for the sake of the gospel. DeYmaz then poses a question, "If Jesus commanded his disciples to go, why did they stay for so long in Jerusalem among their own people?"[37] The reason is because it took them a while to figure out that the Kingdom of God was more far-reaching than the place that they knew, which was just the land within the Jewish borders. Like many of us, they found their current context familiar, and had difficulty leaving that which felt comfortable and normal to them. DeYmaz points to additional areas where we can see the New Testament pattern in the book of Acts, e.g., in Acts 16, where Paul shows us that the church was designed to be the church for all people, both then and now.

The last key to DeYmaz's argument for the call to multi-ethnic ministry, is what he calls the Pauline Mystery. He thinks that the church at Ephesus was a multi-ethnic church.[38] DeYmaz calls this a mystery because it cannot be proven, it is simply based on what is written. Thus Ephesians 1:15-16: "Therefore I also, after I heard of your faith in the Lord Jesus and your love for all the saints, do not cease to give thanks for you, making mention of you in my prayers." The key word in this passage is "all." Who was Paul referencing when he said "all"? DeYmaz believes that he was speaking about the diversity of the people. This

37 DeYmaz, *Building A Healthy Multi-Ethnic Church,* 14.
38 DeYmaz, *Building A Healthy Multi-Ethnic Church,* 19.

is why he calls it a mystery. While DeYmaz does not go deeper into this mystery, he later mentions that diversity is further implied in the book of Revelation. DeYmaz's work brings relevance to the argument that there is a need for multi-ethnic ministry, and that it really is a call from God that can be identified in the Scriptures.

In an earlier collaborative work, DeYmaz and Harry Li suggest that when someone seeks to start the process of mixing diversity into a context where diversity has not been before, they will encounter pushback and rejection.[39] The authors write: "Given the pervasive influence of the homogeneous unit principle (HUP), it is natural to expect a fair amount of pushback or even outright rejection of the multi-ethnic message, regardless of your presentation."[40]

Dan Southerland concurs:

> Anyone who is trying to do something for God will face some opposition. There is always opposition when you lead the church through transition. There will be opposition from those who do not understand the change. There will be opposition from those who understand the change but just don't like it. There will be opposition from those people whose kingdom you are messing with. There will be opposition from those people whom the enemy controls. There will be opposition from those people who just

39 Mark DeYmaz and Harry Li, *Ethnic Blends: Mixing Diversity into your Local Church* (Grand Rapids, MI: Zondervan, 2010).

40 DeYmaz and Li, *Ethnic Blends*, 60.

> love to be contrary. You have each of these groups in your church.[41]

Southerland points out throughout his book that as one attempts to move a church from point A to point B, there will always be people who will try to hold the process back. He warns against allowing that to happen. Southerland writes from a passion to see the church reach its truest potential:

> We are on the edge of a second reformation. The first reformation of the 1500s and 1600s was about the message, about returning to what the bible really says about sin and salivation, about how we relate to God. In the first reformation, the Bible was given back to the people. The second reformation is about the methods. It concerns how we should relate to the world around us; how we make the gospel culturally relevant so that men and women everywhere can come to know, love, and serve Jesus Christ. In this second reformation, the ministry of the church is being given back to the people.[42]

Culture is important to this work. While Southerland speaks about culture and the need to transition effectively, it is also important to take into account the importance of culture. I serve as pastor of an African American church that is transitioning to a multi-ethnic church. This means that we need to be sensitive to

41 Dan Southerland, *Transitioning: Leading your Church Through Change* (Grand Rapids, MI: Zondervan, 1999), 112.

42 Southerland, *Transitioning*, 14-15.

the different cultures that we are seeking to attract. We need to understand the cultures that have walked through and are yet to walk through the doors of the church. Sherwood Lingenfelter writes:

> The complexity of leading cross-culturally lies in the challenge of building a community of trust among people who come from two or more cultural traditions that provoke a clash of worldviews. Because people rely on their cultural understandings for meaning, security and significance, cultural differences have inherent power in human relationships to foster fear and mistrust.[43]

David Anderson, Founding Pastor of Bridgeway Church in Columbia, Maryland, said to me in a conversation that "getting the people to trust you will be your biggest hurdle."[44] I was not sure what he meant by that comment at first, but I later realized that he meant people from different cultures will spend a great deal of time trying to figure out why they should not trust you, and then after they have watched you, listened to you, seen you at work in the ministry, they will begin to trust you in small areas. It is thus a proving process for many. Anderson argues that culture, when it is embraced, can be dealt with correctly from the beginning.

One of the things that has become a force to

---

43 Sherwood G. Lingenfelter, *Leading Cross-Culturally: Covenant Relationships for Effective Christian Leadership* (Grand Rapids, MI: Baker Academic, 2008), 20.

44 Conversation with David Anderson, Bridgeway Church, Columbia, MD, October 10, 2017.

reckon with in African American churches is the issue of control. In history, black people did not have control over their lives, and so when they came into the church and found that it was the one place they had control, they found it difficult to relinquish that control. In many black churches that have been planted, pastors now have complete control. They decide what the agenda will look like and how the money will be spent. It is different when transitioning into a church of many cultures. Southerland points out that there is a risk in releasing control in the church. "A brief review of mission history shows that most mission agencies and missionaries have a great deal of difficulty releasing control." [45] He adds that the risk of letting go is significant.

> Some may judge us to be inept because we have not controlled outcomes that seem essential to process and progress. We ourselves will feel anxiety and stress because the things that we believe are important may not happen in the way that we desire. Releasing control then is an act of faith and trust, both in God and in the person(s) released. The leader who decides to relinquish power is placing trust in the empowered person and in God that the power given will be used to accomplish God's purpose.[46]

Edgar H. Schein helps to put the concept of culture into perspective. Creating culture is a leadership function, he writes, and suggests that culture begins

45 Lingenfelter, *Leading Cross-Culturally*, 128.
46 Lingenfelter, *Leading Cross-Culturally*, 129.

through founder/leader actions. "Cultures basically spring from three sources: 1) The beliefs, values, and assumptions of the founders of organizations; 2) the learning experiences of group members as their organization evolves; and 3) new beliefs, values and assumptions brought in by new members and new leaders."[47]

Schein further states that, "[f]ew organizations form accidentally or spontaneously. They are usually created by one or more individuals who perceive that the coordinated and concerted action of a number or people can accomplish something that individual action cannot. Social movements or new religions begin with prophets, messiahs, or other kinds of charismatic leaders."[48] It becomes clear that in moving one's ministry from being exclusively African American and becoming intentional about welcoming different cultures, one must be prepared and equipped to move in that direction. The questions that come up from time to time include, "What is the current culture of the church? Is the culture one that is welcoming? Is it one that is friendly? Are the people open to change and will everyone's voice be heard? Will everyone benefit from this type of worship style? What really is the current culture?"

Samuel R. Chand writes:

> Culture—not vision or strategy—is the most powerful factor in any organization. It determines the receptivity of staff and volunteers

---

47 Edgar H. Schein, *Organizational Culture and Leadership* (San Francisco, CA: Jossey-Bass, 2010), 219.

48 Schein, *Organizational Culture and Leadership*, 219.

> to new ideas, unleashes or dampens creativity, builds or erodes enthusiasm, and creates a sense of pride or deep discouragement about working or being involved there. Ultimately the culture of an organization—particularly in churches and nonprofit organizations, but also in any organization—shapes individual morale, teamwork, effectiveness and outcomes.[49]

Chand provides assistance in uncovering the nature of an existing culture and identifying the steps of change, by examining the full range of cultural health, from inspiring to toxic. He describes the seven keys of culture as: Control, Understanding, Leadership, Trust, Unafraid, Responsive and Execution. Having insight into one's existing culture is the first and most crucial step toward change.[50] Chand further suggests that vision statements, strategies and goals are good tools, but they can not compare in importance to dealing with culture. The culture of an organization is the platform upon which to build a strong church or nonprofit.[51]

> For one reason or another, some top leaders have an innate distrust of their staff. Their mode of leadership, then, is to tightly control everything their people do. They may smile while squeezing employees, but their employees don't feel valued when they experience scrutiny and micromanagement. On the

49 Samuel R. Chand, *Cracking Your Church's Culture Code: Seven Keys to Unleashing Vision and Inspiration* (San Francisco, CA: Jossey-Bass, 2011), 2.

50 Chand, *Cracking Your Church's Culture Code*, 3.

51 Chand, *Cracking Your Church's Culture Code*, 11.

> other end of the continuum, a few leaders take a hands-off approach. They think their role is to push the ball and just let it roll wherever it goes. They don't give their staff members direction or feedback, so their people wander around confused and frustrated.[52]

This information helps to get organizations ready for the process of learning and growing its people. It pushes leaders to go deeper in the pursuit of the tools needed to be ready for what challenges they will face.

Are the problems that a white church that is trying to transition to a multi-ethnic context face the same challenges as the black church? The key word here is change. Change does not have a color. Soong-Chan Rah discusses the need to understand a culture of colors. "A central theme for this book will be the emphasis on creating an environment in a local church that fosters multicultural and cross-cultural intelligence. At the same time, there will be specific ways to develop that environment of learning that fosters cultural intelligence."[53] Rah goes on to argue that in order for there to be working cross cultural relationships, there must be some level of cultural intelligence. This refers to the need for some races to go through a process of self-reflection to see whether or not they have had privileges that other races may not have had.

DEVELOPING MULTI-ETHNIC LEADERS

There is a general consensus in the literature that it is difficult it is to lead effectively. Lingenfelter writes,

---

52 Chand, *Cracking Your Church's Culture Code*, 12.

53 Soong-Chan Rah, *Many Colors: Cultural Intelligence for a Changing Church* (Chicago, IL:Moody Publishers, 2010), 14.

"The hard facts are that leading is a very difficult thing to do, and the challenges of leadership usually result in something less than the success to which leaders aspire. Perhaps this is the key reason why we see leadership turnover in the church, university, and government. Leading is simply a difficult and challenging task."[54] Ronald A. Heifetz and Marty Linsky concur:

> To lead is to live dangerously because when leadership counts, when you lead people through difficult change, you challenge what people hold dear-their daily habits, tools, loyalties and ways of thinking-with nothing more to offer perhaps than a possibility. Moreover, leadership often means exceeding the authority you are given to tackle the challenge at hand. People push back when you disturb the personal and institutional equilibrium they know. And people resist in all kinds of creative and unexpected ways that can get you taken out of the game: pushed aside, under minded, or eliminated.[55]

One of the recurring themes in Schein's work is that leadership starts with the leader. Many organizations falter because they have disengaged leadership, leadership that is not in tune with "what is happening now."

Schein writes: "The most powerful mechanisms that founders, leaders, managers and parents have

54 Lingenfelter, *Leading Cross-Culturally*, 129.

55 Ronald A. Heifetz and Marty Linsky, *Leadership On The Line: Staying Alive through the Dangers of Leading* (Boston, MA: Harvard Business Review Press, 2002), 2.

available for communicating what they believe in or care about is what they systematically pay attention to. This can mean anything from what they notice and comment on to what they measure, control, reward and in other ways deal with systematically."[56] It is important to understand that the key to moving a church from one state to another potentially involves many different aspects, and leadership seems to be the key. What is the most effective way to lead this change, and what qualities should the leader possess to be effective in leading this change? Ed Young suggests that being creative in leadership is the only way to get people to follow. When a person is creative, there is a certain relevance that comes along with it. "It would take a mammoth effort to keep the church relevant within a constantly changing culture, while remaining anchored to the fundamentals of our ancient faith. To be quite candid, that is the never-ending challenge of the church."[57] Young suggests that it takes a certain kind of leader to be effective at leading change in the lives of the people that he or she serves. He writes, "These leaders don't try to keep pace with cultural change, they set the pace. Creative leaders are trendsetters for creative change, anticipating people's changing needs within their dynamic environments."[58] Along with being creative, there is the issue of inclusion. When one is looking to develop leadership in the church, people need to employ a leadership style that matches the people the church hopes to attract. The

56 Schein, *Organizational Culture and Leadership*, 237.

57 Edwin B. Young, *The Creative Leader: Unleashing the Power of Your Creative Potential* (Nashville, TN: Broadman & Holman Publishers, 2006), 2.

58 Young, *The Creative Leader*, 2.

church at Antioch provides a helpful illustration of a diverse pastoral leadership team, as recorded in Acts 13:1. DeYmaz writes:

> It is interesting that Luke lists these men not only by name but also by ethnicity. Why was Simeon called Niger? Because he was from Niger, a country located, both then and now, in a sub-Saharan West Africa. And Lucius was from Cyrene, a city near the northern coast of Africa in what is today the country of Libya. Perhaps Lucius was one of the original evangelists and church planters at Antioch mentioned in Acts 11:20 and, therefore, among the first to arrive in Antioch speaking to both Jews and Gentiles.[59]

This explanation helps with understanding the text, and after going back to re-read the scriptural text, it is evident that there was diversity and inclusion in the early church. Leadership was important then and the same holds true today. Moving the ministry from a leadership perspective is important and requires having something to say and making sure that the message is heard by those who will use that message to affect others. Liz Wiseman and Greg McKeown describe two leadership types: "Two of the leaders we studied provided a sharp contrast between these two leadership styles. They both worked for the same company and in the same role. One had the midas touch of a multiplier and the other had the chilling effect of a diminisher." [60]

59 DeYmaz, *Building A Healthy Multi-Ethnic Church*, 24.
60 Elizabeth Wiseman with Greg McKeown, *Multipliers: How The Best*

Leadership needs to be done right. A part of leading is developing people around you and developing teams so that ministry can move forward. Ira van Hilliard, Senior Pastor at New Light Christian Center Church in Houston, Texas, said at a conference in 2015, "If you want to do it all by yourself, then go ahead. You will quickly discover that your reach is not that long. Instead, develop a team that can reach far more than you ever could."[61] This is the reason I have developed a great team of people who will work with me to get this transition completed. In fact, the process will never be complete, but we are starting something that it is hoped will produce great results.

In order to be successful, it is important to keep leadership team and staff on the same page. Larry Osborne shows how having a good team can make or break a ministry that is trying to grow, or even to transition. After making so many mistakes and not being as efficient as I could have been in leading my ministry teams and even my secular team, I sought a resource that would assist me in dotting the I's and crossing the T's of my ministry context. I have always asked the "how to" questions, because I, like most pastors, want an exceptional ministry that will service the needs of the community so that we can all experience heaven on earth. Osborne helps his readers look at leadership teams in a different way. All churches have boards and believe that their leadership styles will work well, and yet do not seem to get the effectiveness that they are

---

Leaders Make Everyone Smarter (New York: HarperCollins Publishers, 2010), 8.

61 Ira Van Hilliard, Senior Pastor, New Light Christian Center Church, Houston, TX Church Development Strategies Conference, October 2015.

seeking. Osborne seeks to put churches back on track, and keep them on track.

As a pastor, it is my desire to have a healthy church, one that will continue to run despite the leader, and early in this process I jotted down three pages of notes about things that I wanted to do better. What I found was many hidden roadblocks that have stunted my growth. After reading Osborne's book I can see how various unwise moves I have made have actually sabotaged our ministry growth. Osborne's seasoned and sage advice has over twenty years of backing, and has served me well. The key learning for me is that Osborne teaches how to build, but more than that, he teaches how to maintain a unified and effective team that will be able to stand during trying times.

Additionally, I have realized that to have a "sticky team," one should not leave things to chance, the expectations must be clear. Things as simple as where one holds meetings and the preparation for these meetings is vitally important. I recently hired two new members for our band at the church and after reading Osborne's book, I was able to effectively set salaries that will work for our context. I have decided that even in a small ministry I want to have a "sticky team." There is too much at stake to do otherwise. As Osborne puts it, "I knew something had to change or we'd never get where God wanted us to go."[62]

While looking at different styles and types of leaders, J. Robert Clinton takes a different approach

62 Larry Osborne, *Sticky Teams* (Grand Rapids, MI: Zondervan Publishers, 2010), 129.

to leadership. He argues that leadership has five different phases, and in phase one, God providentially works foundational items into the life of the leader to be. Personality characteristics, good and bad experiences, and the time context are all used by God. The building blocks are all there, although the structure being built may not clearly be in focus.[63] Clinton writes in a devotional style when he suggests that leadership in its beginning stages is happening even before we are aware of what God is doing in our lives. This stage is also redemptive, in that many of the stages that we face in life are not always as impressive as we might wish them to be. God reminds us that he is a sovereign God and that he will be there for us when we need Him.

The second phase in the growth of a leader focuses on inner growth. This is the phase where an emerging leader usually receives training, and often it is informal training in ministry. The leader to be learns by doing in the context of a local church or Christian organization. The basic models through which he learns are imitation modeling and informal apprenticeships, as well as mentoring.[64] This stage focuses on the leader being in a place where training is taking place outwardly, but in a real sense it is the desire and will of God allowing things to happen inwardly. This stage involves a level of testing, during which Clinton suggests that "leadership potential is being identified and God uses testing experience to develop character.[65]

63 J. Robert Clinton, *The Making of a Leader: Recognizing the Lessons and Stages of Leadership Development* (Colorado Springs, CO: NavPress 1988), 26.

64 Clinton, *The Making of a Leader*, 27.

65 Clinton, *The Making of a Leader*, 27.

As I close this chapter, I would be remiss if I failed to mention one of my favorite authors, Rick Warren, who writes as follows:

> As we saw God conform our decision to begin the church in many, many ways in those early days, we learned an important lesson: Wherever God guides, he provides. If you are a church planter, underline that previous sentence. It will be a great source of comfort and strength in your difficult days. Whatever he calls us to do, he will enable and equip us to do. God is faithful! He keeps his promises.[66]

Warren is speaking about the God factor. Whatever we do, it is up to God to bless it. We must do our part and rely on his grace and favor to open doors for us that we are not able to open for ourselves.

SUMMARY

The research cited in this chapter reveals there is a lot of information available concerning transitioning churches, and that we can learn from the pioneers of the movement. However, there is much more to learn and experience in this area. Moreover, the development of a model for transitioning a church will require adapting and contextualizing ideas that may have worked in a different context and are potentially transferable. The research that I have presented provides core concepts that are important and helpful for any church seeking to transition into a multi ethnic ministry.

---

66 Rick Warren, *The Purpose Driven Church: Growth Without Compromising Your Message and Mission* (Grand Rapids, MI: Zondervan Publishers, 1995), 38.

STEP 3: SURVEYING THE LEADERSHIP/ CONGREGATION

The practical steps described in the next three chapters are based on the method I followed in order to begin to move my own church, More Than Conquerors Worship Center, from being a mono-ethnic to a multi-ethnic church. In the suggestions made, and the method recommended, More Than Conquerors functions as a case study. I appreciate Robert K. Yin's remarks about using this method to answer the how and why questions. Yin offers the following description of a case study, "A case study is an empirical inquiry that investigates a contemporary phenomenon within its real-life context, especially when the boundaries between phenomenon and context are not clear."[67]

My chosen model was the redemptive model, which is a model that points to the need to look at competencies, principles, character, and finally the transformation that takes an organization to the redemptive stage.

As I sought to gain qualitative and quantitative information about how this might be achieved, I decided that the type of methodology that would give me the results that I was seeking should consist in the first place of a survey and questionnaires. (These would be followed by teaching programs on inclusiveness and practical applications of that teaching in the form of outreach to the community in which the church is situated.) The helpfulness of this approach prompts me to recommend it as the basis for those seeking to make a similar transition in their churches.

It takes time to gather the information needed to implement the transition to a multi-ethnic church (in my case it was collected over a six-month period). When seeking to transition their churches, pastors might wish to pose similar questions that I posed and take the time to explain to the leadership and the congregation where it is they want to take their church. They will need to teach their congregation and then request that the church follow them in the process. It is necessary to take the time to study the mindset

---

67 Robert K. Yin, *Case Study Research: Design and Methods* (Thousand Oaks, CA Sage Publications, 2003), 13.

of the partners/church members from the awareness that one cannot not drive them to think or feel a certain way.

During the period I was following this method at More than Conquerors, I planned to meet with our members in a group setting and then interview them individually to ensure that what was presented in the group setting was echoed in the personal interviews. I was interested in gathering information about what they thought about us moving forward and intentionally opening up to and inviting people from other cultures to be a part of our church. This I think an indispensable first step in the transitioning process.

As a part of this study, I planned to conduct a teaching series to be followed up with interviews, both individual interviews and group interviews. I also planned to canvas the congregation for their thoughts to see if they affirmed the move towards inclusiveness in our church journey.

I decided to do this research for people across the world who have a sense that God no longer wants us to be the African American church, or the Caucasian church, or the Asian church, but one church that comes together to worship and glorify God.

I wanted the group to be clear about what the goal was, so that they did not feel this was just an assignment that their pastor wanted them to carry out. I thus planned on having teaching sessions, individual meetings, and group fellowship over coffee and hot dogs over the course of six months to collect data.

I planned to have surveys on hand and have a different person in the group collect and score/process them. I wanted to take myself out of the data collection phase to give the process integrity. The survey participants consisted of the church leadership as well as members of the church.

I decided to hold different sessions for leaders and volunteers as there would be different expectations on leadership in terms of things that are required of them. I anticipated that some of the potential problems during this process might be that people would not be as interested, either inside our current church or in the community. People are often afraid of change or have decided that they will not be a part of any change. I was also concerned that some in our congregation might take offense and want to know why the pastor was doing this. I anticipated some would think that we were fine as we are.

Every process must start somewhere. Stephen Covey writes: "Each decision we make is an important decision. Some may seem small at the time, but the reality is that they add upon one another to become habits of the heart that move us with increasing force toward some destiny."[68] We started this process with the understanding that it would take us somewhere, that it would lead us toward our destiny.

I cannot minimize the amount of prayer and fasting that has gone into getting us to the point where we are now. We have had unconventional prayer gatherings at six in the mornings as well as daily prayer

68 Stephen R. Covey, A. Roger Merrill and Rebecca R. Merrill, *First Things First* (New York: Simon & Schuster, 1994), 296.

Monday through Friday on a conference call line. I was completely dependent on God to move in the lives of the people to catch the vision and to seek also to move the ministry forward in this fashion. In what follows I describe the process used to gain information from key leadership in the congregation, which was the first phase of the transition.

THE SURVEY

I conducted a survey of ministers on my staff as well as ministry leaders and youth leaders. I chose these particular people because I wanted to be sure that I was getting information that would be unchecked and unhindered by any negative forces. I wanted people to tell me the truth and not just answer the way that they thought I might want them to answer. I wanted people I knew would keep it real for me. After my team and I had discussed and developed the questions—which took several weeks because we sought information that would be useful—we developed the process for gathering the data.

It is important that such a process have as much integrity as possible and so it is helpful if someone other than the pastor oversees the process. Thus in our case I assured the respondents that at no time would I see their responses, and hence made it clear that I did not want them to copy me in on the responses by accident. I wanted the members who were being surveyed to feel comfortable that their pastor was not going to be looking over their shoulders and trying to manage the process.

We asked twelve questions designed to reach a full understanding of where the leaders stood in relation to creating a different worship culture, but more than that, to reach an understanding of how they approached cultural diversity, and the questions we asked were as follows. In other contexts the questions might need to be different, and the survey adapted in other ways, but I provide them here as a starting point.

1. What is your age?
2. Are you male or female?
3. Do you believe in and support community worship?
4. Would you be willing to assist someone from another race/culture feel comfortable at our church?
5. Would you be willing to go outside of the walls of the church to do intentional evangelism in the Caucasian, Hispanic, and Asian communities surrounding our church?
6. Would you welcome and support cultural diversity at our church?
7. Would you be open to having white, Asian, and Hispanic persons join our church?
8. If we were to have small group Bible studies and you were assigned to a group where the leader was from a diverse cultural group, would you:
    a. still participate?
    b. be comfortable participating?

   c. feel comfortable sharing your heart in that setting? What do you consider to be the general theme of Matthew 6:10?

4. Would you support MTCWC being very intentional about welcoming African American, Caucasian, Asian, Hispanic, and Native Americans to worship with us?
5. Would you support having a diverse staff, leadership and/or worship leader?
6. Would you just like everything to stay the same?

I was grateful that the leadership team cared for me and trusted me enough to assist me with this survey. The survey had been created to draw out people's thoughts on a redemptive process. The results were very positive. Of the respondents, 80% were overall wholeheartedly supportive. I was overwhelmed by the fact that in most of the responses people supported the transition to a multi-ethnic church. They understood "the ask" and they responded positively.

From a "principle" perspective, (i.e., looking at the underlying truths which transcend situations), they answered the survey questions from the standpoint of what was important to them. Many had previously shared with me that they were raised to dislike other races and had stayed close to the race they are a part of because of false information growing up. Many also shared during our live sessions, which I will discuss later, that they had been to churches that preached the black message only, and found it rewarding and refreshing to find a ministry like More Than Conquerors that was welcoming and inclusive. Their responses were clear that what they once thought had been superseded by where they are now. It blessed me to see that they have allowed the influence of the Word of God to move them forward in the things of God.

At various levels I am starting to see the impact that this process is having in the lives of our congregation and leadership teams.

Stephen Covey remarked at a leadership summit that, "principles are guidelines for human conduct that are proven to have enduring permanent value."[69] I am looking for the enduring permanent value that this process will have in the lives of not only More Than Conquerors, but the community of Edgewood and Harford County, Maryland. At every level of our lives, we need to see and know that something is working, changing, and impacting the overall good of the process. Take minute before we move forward to look at where you are. You have identified the process that you want to move forward with, and now you are doing the work. Even if only in small ways, you should begin or have begun to see some fruit from what you are working on. When we set out to lose weight, we make a decision and start working. We gather up the right food to eat and we decide to start a workout regimen. After two weeks of drinking water and protein drinks couples with fewer carbs and more protein and two walks a say and strength training in the gym, we should start to see some results. Now, we need to

69 Stephen R. Covey, Leadership Summit, Marriott Corporation, June 1995.

understand that the word "results" is relative. It means different things to different people. We start off small even though we serve a BIG God, although we do not have to think or start small. Nonetheless we need to see results. This what I started seeing at this point with my teams. They were motivated and started taking steps to be welcoming that I did not teach them or even ask them to do. They would create avenues to be kind. They were mindful and yet mind full at the same time. What's the difference, you ask? Mind full is future focused and mindful is "how" focused. They were thinking about how to get things done and how that would affect the future of our church. I loved it. They were focused and I was a proud Pastor because of it.

I was able to ascertain from the survey that my leadership operated with character. According to Rodney Cooper, of Gordon Conwell, character "involves both our pluses and minuses, our strengths and vulnerabilities; it involves identifying and beginning to face our dark side." The survey tool showed me that there were still some who had reservations about moving forward, as 80 percent expressed their enthusiasm for moving forward and could not wait to see the fullness of the vision come to pass. But 20 percent stated they would prefer things to stay the same, and did not see the need for change. and while twelve said no, lets change, three said that they did want things to stay the same. They were not all interested in becoming a multi-ethnic church. In fact, one respondent said that she would leave the church if we continued down this path. This individual said that the black church had become the black church for a reason. It was a place where she felt safe and could be who God called her to be. She did not want to come to church and have to "put on a front for some white people." She shared that she would not do it and if I continued down this path, she would not continue her membership at More Than Conquerors Worship Center. While I expected to have some push back, I did not expect the push back to come from my leadership or for it to be so harsh. I shared the results with the leadership team the next week and told them that I had to do what God had called me to do, and that it was acceptable if any of them felt the new direction that we planned to move in as a ministry did not fit their values. I was comfortable with them leaving the ministry. I then asked them to give me ninety days to share the teachings with the congregation and they could then evaluate where they were at that point. They all agreed. Now, I do need to say to you that when you decide to move forward for your own personal growth, mental capacity and emotional wellbeing, not everyone will be excited or happy, and in short, some folks will not want to go with you. You must get to a place where you are fine with that, and have a mind made-up that says, "I will go with the goers. I will not hate you, talk about you, embarrass you through preaching." In the black church we call it preaching "on you." Please do not do that. Love them enough to let them go. You cannot change your focus because not everyone sees things from your level. In the book of Nehemiah 8:4, Ezra has to stand on a stage, higher than the people, because his assignment is different. He needs to be able to see higher than the people he is ministering to. Sometimes you are called to a higher place simply because God knows that you will need to see at a different level. Understand that when you are at that level, some folks will want you to always be on their level and will not understand when you have to leave them to go higher. Yet that is what Conquerors need to do!

I appreciated those comments as they helped me to understand where the challenges might be, and that I might thus find ways, through intentional preaching and teaching, to emphasize the need for change and the need for inclusiveness. I was clear when I started this process that I had to come to a new understanding of both Scripture and how I was leading my congregation. I had to ask the difficult question about what God thought of my inability to speak on the need to be inclusive. I thus appreciated the truth that was reflected in the survey. It showed that the respondents had character and they wanted their voice to be heard. Bill Thrall once said, "Honesty is telling others the truth; Integrity is telling ourselves the truth." The respondents were true to themselves and that made me proud.

The redemptive model has a transformative component that is life changing. Rodney Cooper remarked once that a transformational leader is one who will, "focus on heart change, or deep change in themselves, their followers and the organization, [and who] understands that meaningful and lasting change occurs from the inside out." I saw transformational responses in the survey. I saw that the people being surveyed took this transformation of our ministry to heart and realized that there is a need for change in our congregation. What is more incredible is seeing that this process has changed them on the inside.

The final phase of the redemptive model involves leaders becoming redemptive. According to Cooper, redemptive leaders influence "those whom they touch to significantly experience God's redemptive power in their lives so that they may be unleashed to live life to their full potential. Redemptive leaders guide others into finding and releasing the power of their own redemptive stories in their successes, failures, wounds, and tragedies. They, then, are powerfully able to speak hope and healing, by God's grace, into the hearts of others."

What I gained from the survey was that I pastored a church that is redemptive.

THE CONGREGATION WANTED TO DO THE RIGHT THINGS FOR THE RIGHT REASONS. AND MOST OF ALL, THEY WANTED

TO GROW AND HELP THE NEXT PERSON DO BETTER SO THAT WE COULD CHANGE THE WORLD, ONE COMMUNITY AT A TIME.

I have pastored now for fifteen years, and one of the things that I have learned is that if you want to know something, just ask the people. When you develop relationships with people and genuinely love people, you will want to communicate with them. I know too many pastors who do not like their members, and because of bad experiences in church they have allowed their hearts to grow hard towards the members. The story is told of a mother who went to wake her son for church one Sunday morning. When she knocked on his door, he said, "I'm not going!" "Why not?" asked his mother. "I'll give you two good reasons," he replied. "One, they don't like me. Two, I don't like them." His mother replied, "I'll give you two good reasons why you *will* go to church. One, you're 47 years old. Two, you're the pastor."

I know that leading people is not an easy task, but if God calls you to it, He has a plan for you. Just ask the people. They will tell you. I remember one season I wanted to hold a revival. We had never had a revival before, but it was the "churchy" thing to do. I called a friend of mine and asked him to come preach at my three-day revival and he agreed. But my members did not support it. I was very frustrated. When I pulled them together to ask why they did not support the revival, they said, "We don't come to nothing at night." "It is too bad around here," added one of the members. She then said something that changed my life: "You should have asked us, we would have told you that we were not coming. I learned that day to ask them, so that I will not be frustrated when they won't come out. Ask your people the questions and they will tell you what you need to know. I no longer do anything in my church without first running it past my team.

STEP 4: PREPARING THE CONGREGATION

I announced to the church the vision that God had given me on the first Sunday in June 2015, and I have not stopped talking about it since. Every Sunday and every Wednesday I speak about inclusiveness and I share the changes that are taking place through our *Weekly Voice* magazine. We use Facebook, Instagram, and Twitter to communicate internally and externally. We have developed C-Groups that are small groups led by one of the leaders of the ministry. I teach the entire congregation on Sundays and Wednesdays and my C-Groups meet on Thursdays and Saturdays. This is a small group concept that we use for fellowship and for sharing information along with the Word of God. I believe that every opportunity should be a teaching opportunity and that we should never come together without some form of the Word being shared to the group. The small group method, as well as the large group method, followed up with the *Weekly Voice* magazine has proven very successful. Social media allows for immediate responses from my social media minister for that week. Every leader takes a week to respond to questions and they are also responsible for sharing content to our cyber congregation. We have a large cyber congregation on Periscope that is a part of our church. We value them and have made them partners of the ministry.

We have been doing on-line church for a little over a year, and we have grown. However, we might not have survived as a church had we not embraced social media technology prior to the pandemic. We taught our congregation how to get on Facebook and YouTube. I had to show them how to go to the Zoom Room for fellowship at the completion of regular services. I held virtual pizza parties with my teens on zoom and purchased the pizzas for each young person. We used Google hangout to host women's events as well. Businesses were able to grow from using social media and I organized a new website that allowed us to post study guides for Bible studies also.

THE TEACHING SERIES

Standing on the Word of God that is shared in Matthew 28:19 I pulled key leadership and the entire church together for four weeks to teach a series on the biblical basis for multi-ethnic churches. The text reads: "Go ye therefore, and teach all nations, baptizing them in the name of the Father, and of the Son, and of the Holy Ghost," (Matthew 28:19, KJV).

The following teaching series, which is the one we used, is provided as a guide, as a source of ideas - as something to use, adapt, or take as a starting point:

The first teaching session in the series was called "The Power of One: Cultivating Strong Relationships," and can be summarized as follows: Jesus is ministering to the Samaritan women with her water pot. They enter dialogue and Jesus is able to change this women with a conversation, so much so that the women go and tells everyone that she knows about this man (John 4: 21-39). Our responsibility as believers is to tell someone about the Lord, for Jesus said go and share my word with another.

Acts 1:8 also indicates it is our individual responsibility to share the gospel. In our generation God will use each of us to reach even one person. If we think about it, we could double the attendance in one week if everyone brought just one person.

This particular teaching thus focused on the discovery of the Power of One, and the dynamics and the demonstration of the Power of One. Some examples of the Power of One that were shared in the teaching include:

1. Mary was one woman who was ready and able to be used to perform a miracle.

2. Joseph was one-man God used to be there for his family despite all the persecution he had endured.
3. Esther was one woman who spoke a word of salvation for her people.
4. David was one man God used to rally the people and to kill the giant.
5. Abraham was one man to whom the revelation of faith was given. The Bible says that he is the father of us all.
6. Moses too was one man. God does not give His vision to a committee, but to a single committed person. Thousands of people depended on Moses to go to Pharaoh with a word from the Lord, saying "Let my people go."
7. We are all are important to the plan of God. God placed us where we are because we have a purpose?

The second message was called "The Power of Barrier Breaking Faith (It Ain't Going Down Like This)" and was based on John 5:2-9. The contents of this teaching can be summarized as follows: This lesson was designed to get rid of barriers that keep people from getting all that God has for them, and it was designed to help people discover what is preventing them from having God's best.

The main points that were drawn from the passage in John were as follows:

1. The man in John's narrative has had a frustrating condition for thirty-eight years.

2. There are a lot of people who are sick.
3. When the water moves or bubbles, healing is available.
4. This man has been there so long, just waiting for the bubbling.
5. One-day Jesus walks up and asks, "Do you want to be made whole?"
6. The man is so concerned about the bubbling water that he does not realize who he is talking to.
7. He has allowed what he knows and what he has experienced to stand in his way and become a barrier.
8. The lesson from this is we need to identify barriers and then use faith to get rid of them.
9. For every faith obstacle there is a barrier assigned to prevent reaching the results.
10. Jesus is trying to get this man to focus on his deliverance and not the pool.
11. Jesus is trying to get the man to rid himself of excuses (the reason why I can't do it, I can't do it because of this and that).
12. The message of faith is about attacking that which has come to overtake us.

The third sermon was entitled "The Power of His Presence" and was largely based on Psalm 16:1-10. The message of this Psalm is designed to get believer and non-believer alike to understand that waiting on God is not bad, although in many instances, we are not waiting on God at all. We have found that he has allowed us to be where we are, thus reaching an understanding that

God knows what we are facing, and he will then show His glory. There are those of us who need to be reinvigorated in our praise and worship, and reanimated in our desire to be in His presence. Any of us, if we are not careful, can slip into an Ephesus church mentality clothed in Revelation, something I talked about in a prior message to the congregation. An Ephesus mentality involves doing Godly stuff without an intimate fellowship with God. One would have to list the author of Psalm 16 as one of the top worshippers in the Bible. David's whole persona exudes worship. Not only does he worship, he is a worshipper. In this message, special emphasis was placed on how to worship. When we are waiting, our mentality should be that of a worshipper, not just someone going through the motions. This Psalm is a celebration of the joy of fellowship that David realizes comes from faith in the Lord. It may have been written when David faced great danger in the wilderness or opposition in his reign. Whatever its cause, David was convinced that because he had come to know and trust the Lord as his portion in life, he could trust Him in the face of death.

With all that is going on in the world with politics, and "black lives matter," racial division, bills on the rise, income not moving, police officers being killed, I have a suspicion somebody could use some encouragement, and who better to encourage us than the sweet hymnist of Israel, King David?

The last message that I shared during this month of inclusion was entitled "The Power of Choice," and was preached from Ephesians 4:25-27 (NASB).

"Therefore, laying aside falsehood, speak truth each one of you with his neighbor, for we are members of one another. Be angry, and yet do not sin; do not let the sun go down on your anger, and do not give the devil an opportunity." This message was designed to point out to the congregation that they have a choice, and that if they will follow the Word of God for their lives and make the choice to move the kingdom forward, they will live in their best days. We looked at the church at Ephesus to see how Paul ministered, and what he was talking about in verse 25.

We asked and answered the following questions: What falsehood should be laid aside according to verse 25? What did Paul mean when he said that we are members of one another? Does Paul give us permission to be angry in verse 26? Who should we be angry with? With white people? Why are we angry? How can I work to let some things go from my history? Why am I angry? Can I be happy? Are Hispanics the reason that I am angry? Why do I get angry at what I may not understand? What did Paul mean?

At the end of this teaching session, each member was encouraged to find one person in the church and decide that they would connect two times before the next service. They were at this point well equipped, because I had been teaching on evangelism in Bible study on Wednesday, and this was their call to action.

SUMMARY

This process of beginning the work that as a congregation we had been talking about for almost a year was exciting and rewarding at the same time. Our congregation grabbed the vision and decided to run with it. These members were selected because they were the ones God called to help me start and complete this work. They were effective in helping form the redemptive leadership model and putting in the time to do the work. They understood that to achieve the transformation desired they would have to stand on the frontline to help bring the message to those who would come after we had started the process. They understood that not every leader in the church, not every member, and not every community partner would get on board. They were trained to expect difficulties ahead, but we decided that we would win with the hand that we had been dealt. The team was committed to walking the vision through and determined to follow the strategy that had been designed, and that we were implementing, so that More Than Conquerors Worship could become the thriving multi-ethnic church that God was calling us to be.

From a non-church perspective, what are you doing to prepare the people around you for the change that is coming? Have you asked questions about the support that you are looking for? Have you solicited help from people to help you get to where you want to go? Have you taken steps to get rid of naysayers and negative people? Have you gotten the Lissa's and the Andre's out of your circle? Have you made peace with yourself and given yourself permission to grow and be great? Prepare now! Decide that you will no longer watch everyone else be great while you sit by and have a woulda-shoulda-coulda pity party. Decide today that your yes is out there, and keep looking for it until it becomes your reality.

STEP 5: ENGAGING THE COMMUNITY

The purpose of this book is to apply the redemptive leadership model to transforming a local congregation into a multi-ethnic congregation as well as pushing every reader to become a Conqueror. The particular church involved was More Than Conquerors Worship Center, but the lessons learned can be applied in any congregation wishing to become multi-ethnic in their composition.

Growing numbers of churches are being planted, and many of their founder's desire to be multi-ethnic, and so they start off that way. The founders plant a multi-ethnic church, or they plant a white church or a Hispanic church, and that is what the church becomes. At the same time, there are white congregations that have a desire to diversify their existing ministries and accordingly they begin the process of becoming multi-ethnic. This is not the norm for the African American community. The black church is something of an institution: it is often considered a safe place, a gathering facility where people can go to get away from the world and its pressures and feel comfortable just being who they are. The questions pastors of black churches need to address are: "Why do you want to transform an African American church into a multi-ethnic church? In what way are you hoping to benefit by doing this?" These are just two of the questions that I, as well as my ministry team, have been asked during the two years we have been intentional about diversifying our ministry.

In conducting this diversification strategy, I started with a plan that involved inviting and empowering my leadership team to come on this journey with me. I shared the vision and what I sensed God was calling me to do. The team had many questions, but they trusted me and my leadership. I began to share with the church that I had a witness from God to do things differently in moving the church forward. I shared on a Sunday morning in June that we would begin the process of transforming our ministry, so that people who were different from us would feel welcome. I asked the following:

"If you have white friends or family, stand up."
"If you have Hispanic friends or family, stand up."
"If you have Native American friends or family, stand up."
"If you have Asian friends or family, stand up."

At this point, with about eighty people in the room, every person in the congregation was standing. Everyone was black in the room, but everyone knew people from other races, or had family members from other races. People socialized with other races, partied with them, and ate with them, but for some reason, in this church, did not worship with them. It was at that point that I realized many of the members were also hungry for change and wanted to create an atmosphere where the people they socialize with might be welcome. It was at this point that MTC became very intentional about the direction that our church would move in.

PRACTICAL STEPS TO BECOMING MULTI-ETHNIC

EXPANDING THE NETWORK

With my leadership team on board, we needed to make some immediate changes, both internally and externally. We wanted to maintain our external relationships with the African American community; however, we wanted to add some new relationships that complemented where we were going. We thus became a member of Joel Osteen's Champions Network, which gave us national exposure. Additionally, we joined Mosiaxx Global network and started interacting with pastors and churches that were already making the changes things that we wanted to make. I also realized that I needed to find a pastor/mentor who could speak into my life and with whom my wife would also feel comfortable. We searched and finally found a suitable pastor and his lady , and so we joined the Sheppard's Connection under Dr. R A Vernon and Lady Victory Vernon from The Word Church in Cleveland, OH, and their input has been extremely helpful.

ASSESS WORSHIP PRACTICES

As far as internal change went, we decided we needed to be very intentional about our worship services and ask a series of questions designed to make us more welcoming to other cultures. How long should the praise and worship continue? Who would follow on the stage after praise and worship? Who would be at the door? Who would be in the parking lot? Who would be the greeters? We had to train and retrain every ministry to have a welcoming spirit, and stress that the way we hug our black partners would be the way we would hug our white, Hispanic, and Asian partners. We decided that we would no longer call the people in our church "members," we would call them "partners." Anyone could be a member, but we were looking for people who would partner with us in order to create something transformative and redemptive in the Edgewood community. We thought that if we got the internal workings of the church right and made the internal aspects of the church attractive, we would feel good about inviting people to come to our worship. We wanted to make sure that people were greeted as soon as they arrived on the property in the parking lot and that there would be someone holding the door open when that guests arrived. We no longer called our guests visitors; they became guests in our home. Every area had to be made ready for the experience. We no longer used the word service, but we started using the word "experience." Every greeter would say, "Welcome to More Than Conquerors, enjoy the experience." We wanted people to have a memorable experience so that they would return.

Our worship changed for the better. It was something of what we already had, and we added some elements that made for a better experience. We added a bass guitar player and we also added a paid worship leader. We had neither of these before. We became very intentional about timeliness in worship and being comfortable shutting some things down and opening other things up. We decided that we would move by the Holy Spirit in worship, and so we got rid of the programs. We did not want to be held captive by a program. We are sensitive to the Holy Spirit and if the glory falls while we are in praise and worship, then the glory falls. If the glory falls during our time of prayer, that is where we will end. Some Sundays there is no preached Word if the glory falls at another time in the experience. Thus, worship changed, but it was enhanced. We have received very positive feedback from guests and current partners about how good the worship felt, and how in many instances, it was life changing.

We heard from our white brothers and sisters that they appreciated the feeling of warmth, and from the black brothers and sisters we heard appreciation for our praise and worship, including the addition of a bass guitar player and white praise team members. That being said, we also heard that our music was much too loud, so we are trying to make adjustments there as well. We have not heard much from the few Hispanic guests that come to our services. They have been visiting but have shared that until we get a Hispanic translator they will not join. We are searching for such a person to join our team, but at time of writing have not yet been successful.

WHO SHOULD YOU TARGET?

As noted in Chapter 1, census data from 2000 showed that 68.10 percent of the population in the community were white, 25.66 percent black, 0.4 percent native American, 1.6 percent Asian and 3.4 percent Hispanic.[70] This was our starting point. We realized quickly that we wanted to look at the white community as they were the largest, but we also wanted to attract black families. We knew that the Asian and Hispanic populations were small, but we still wanted to find out where there were so that we could target them as well. Additionally, we learned that of the population in total, 32.2 percent were under eighteen, 9 percent were between eighteen and twenty-four, 33 percent were between twenty-five and forty-four, 19.6 percent were between forty-five and sixty-four. with

70 Wikipedia, "Edgewood, Maryland," last accessed February 1, 2019 https://en.wikipedia.org/ wiki/Edgewood-Maryland.

6.3 percent being sixty-five and older. This helped a great deal, as we were attracting people from all these groups, but we really wanted the 33 percent that were between twenty-five and forty-four. as that was the age group of the pastor and the leaders. Our focus was on the white population and the Hispanic population. We started going on walks through the community and talking to people about where people go to socialize in Edgewood. We developed relationships with the one high school, the two middle schools and the three elementary schools. We attended events at the school, we partnered with the school to meet the children. We started doing after school tutoring programs and developed excellent relationships with the school leadership. They viewed us as partners, as we would adopt families throughout the year, and we would adopt a classroom every month and purchase pizza for that classroom once a month. This was a small investment that had a tremendous impact on our ability to be relevant in the community. Children started telling their parents and the parents wanted to come and see what was so exciting about this church. While in the schools we found out about after-school programming in the community that included football, basketball, and lacrosse games. We went to those games and spoke to people about connecting with us. We would use these events as the opportunity to share a little about our church and ask people if they would give us ninety minutes of their time on Sundays. We told them that we would even give them free food after the experience and many of them agreed to do so. This started us on our way in deciding who to target. The twenty-five to forty-four age group worked well for us because many of the children in the under eighteen group were the children of those we were targeting.

EVANGELIZE IN THE COMMUNITY

One of the priorities that our leadership team discussed was to immediately start teaching the congregation why we should be inclusive, drawing on the Word of God. I decided that we would teach our partners and potential guests at the same time, so that we all heard the same message. This practice would present opportunities for fellowship and we would receive immediate feedback on the experience. To further this objective, at one of our weekly leadership team meetings, one of the leaders said, "Why don't we go out and evangelize on Saturday before the teachings on Sunday and invite people to come to church?" The team discussed this and saw it as an opportunity to connect with the community, let them know about our presence in the area, and extend an open invitation for them to come and be a part of our community. As we prepared to go out into the broader community, I provided brief teachings on lifestyle evangelism to my leadership team and the young people in our church. I taught evangelism at 10 a.m. on Saturday mornings and then we would go out at noon. As a result of this teaching, they knew what to say, when to talk and when to listen. The team was very excited about this outreach to the community. On Friday nights we would have a rally to galvanize the team and get everyone excited about Saturday's teachings as well as about the evangelism opportunity. On our first Saturday, eighteen people came to the training and they all participated in our evangelism efforts. After training we loaded up the vans and went to the location where we had decided to canvas. After prayer in the community, we set the ground rules that no one was to go about alone and that we would ring a bell whenever someone was saved. It was an awesome experience. We gave away water bottles with our labels on that read: "Come and Enjoy the Experience." It was a hot day, and everyone enjoyed a refreshing bottle of water. The first weekend we went to the Hispanic trailer park. We knocked on doors and spoke to people in their driveways. We had on shirts that said iServe and we told people that we were in the area to serve. We asked if there was anything that we could help them with and although many said no, others allowed us to move items, take out trash and some even asked for prayer. We were surprised at the number of people who wanted us in that community. We ministered salvation to six people and invited forty people to come to our experience on Sunday. People told us that they would indeed come to church on Sunday. Many needed directions and others needed rides. We made sure that we had all the contact information on hand and we ended our time in that Hispanic community at 2 p.m.

On Sunday we were ready to see the harvest that would result from our efforts and one of the families we had met on Saturday came to our experience. We were so excited to welcome them as our guests. Everyone hugged them and made sure that they were comfortable and after our worship experience we went outside for a fellowship around hotdogs and chips. We were able to get to know this family and we shared a meal together. We followed the same process for the next two weeks, targeting the white community and the African American community. We had more than twenty guests during those three weeks, and three families joined our congregation. The word was now out that More Than Conquerors Worship Center was a church for all people.

WHAT WE LEARNED

We learned that people are hungry for the Word of God in every community that we visited. People are looking for a safe place to worship and fellowship. We learned that people are no longer looking for "church as usual," but are looking for substantial teaching and authentic praise and worship and they want it in a timely manner. We learned that people are not interested in staying in church all day. We learned that people are looking for Christian education opportunities while they are in church so that their children will be fed as well. We learned that white people like to have a band and blacks and Hispanics like the choir praise team style of worship. We learned that white people come to church ten to fifteen minutes early and black and Hispanic people come either right on time or ten to fifteen minutes late. We monitored this over a three-month period, and it remained consistent.

Our major learnings were that people were very open to community worship and in many cases, the ethnicity of the worshipper did not matter. We also learned from our hotdog and chip fellowships that many Hispanic people do not go to non-Hispanic churches, because in many cases they do not understand what is going on. Many do not know English and so they shy away from what is unfamiliar or incomprehensible. One of the Hispanic guests shared that if we had an interpreter and he could understand the teachings, he would come every week. Another guest shared that our experience moves too fast, and we need to slow it down. Several of the white guests said that they felt welcome and that there was a warm spirit in the church. Our black guests shared that they enjoyed the personal invitation, they enjoyed the food, and the fact that we play basketball in the gym on Sunday after the experience. Not only did we receive feedback from our community guests, we wanted to hear from our partners as well. They came one by one to say that they felt good and one of the youth shared that he was so excited that he could now invite his girlfriend to church. I asked why now, and he said, "because my girlfriend is white and now we both will feel comfortable. She will feel comfortable because she will know that our pastor is a cool dude and he wants the church to be multi-ethnic and me because it is no longer a secret that I date a white girl." That comment overwhelmed me, as I had no idea that my teens thought like that. I thought that they knew their pastor well enough to know that I am a lover of all people. This key learning was most important for me: people do not always know everything about you. In many cases there is so much ambiguity, people do not know how to enter different or difficult conversations. People are looking for a leader to be authentic and once they feel this is the case, they begin the process of letting you in to their innermost being. Leadership expert Susan Scott puts it like this: "Authenticity is not something you have; it is something you choose."[71]

PRECONDITIONS FOR SUCCESS

As a result of what we learned through the process at More than Conquerors, I identify the following three things you need for success:

You will need open minds: The congregation needs a yes in their spirit and not a focus on what cannot be done. In our case, I wanted people to be willing to be exposed to things that they had not been exposed to before. I wanted them to leave their comfort zones and intentionally engage with people from other races. I asked them to be willing to approach guests and share the love of Christ. I needed them to be open about sowing new seeds, so that the ministry could do extra outreach and evangelism. I was asking them to have open minds so that we could all grow together.

You will need people with a willingness to learn. I asked the leadership to attend a two-month Bible study where I taught inclusiveness and faith. I required

71 Susan Scott, *Fierce Conversations: Achieving Success at Work and in Life, One Conversation at a Time* (New York: The Berkley Publishing Group, 2004), 68.

that if they were going to embark on this journey, they needed to be present and not miss a class. We decided that we would all be each other's accountability partners and we would not have a problem holding each other accountable. My goal through the teaching was to share in a small group the Word of God and then have a practical application time where we could put the Word to good use. There were books that I asked everyone to purchase that served as our guide as we started our process. These were *First Things First* by Stephen R. Covey, *Sticky Teams* by Larry Osborne and *Building a Healthy Multi-Ethnic Church* by Mark DeYmaz. In addition to coming for Bible study with me every Saturday, there was required reading from the books that I listed. During the lesson time, I would challenge them to discuss the chapter we had read and tell me their thoughts. I began seeing a passion for this type of work and we all repented that we had not started this process earlier.

You will need people with a willingness to serve. I wanted to develop and create a team that would be on fire for the things of God. I wanted them to understand that God needs our hands and our feet in this world, and that if we were going to change the world one community at a time, then the time was now and we were the people to bring about inclusion in our community. I wanted the team to be ready to work at a minute's notice. I wanted them to understand why we were working. What we found was that while we thought we were out helping the community to become one, we were the ones getting blessed. We realized that it was our pleasure to serve. It was at that point that we started to realize what a privilege it is to serve in this way. I taught the team that God could have chosen anyone to do this work, and the fact that he had chosen us is a privilege. I thus asked for a willingness to serve and people understood that God did not have to choose us, but he had, and we wanted to please Him. I would share with them that "when my heart is right towards God, and my desire is to please God, it obligates him to bring me in the company of the people that I need to know and the knowledge of the things that I need to know so that my path is relevant." In other words, I shared with them that what we do for other people, we do for God. His promise is that He will reward us.

You will need compassion for others: I would spend my Saturday evenings with different families of my leadership. One week we would eat at Cracker Barrell, another Saturday we would meet at Taco Love Grill, but I wanted to hear in a private setting their heart for God and the ministry that we were called to. I was looking for compassion for other people and the desire to grow people and watch God appear in their lives. As we sat in these restaurants, I listened to them share what the process had been like for them, and perhaps identify a family or a person they had ministered to. They articulated their passion for loving people and showing people the way of the Lord. They shared the salvation stories of people they had led to Christ. They were doing exactly what I had asked of them. They were showing that they cared and that they wanted us to be intentional about not allowing the passion for this work to die after my thesis-project was complete. We would all sit and cry together and would end up being in the restaurant in worship and adoration for God's goodness. If I needed another sign, this was it: the hand of God is on this work and on His people.

CONCLUSION

At the start, success was defined as our team doing its best to change the way that the church views inclusion and share that with others. If their minds and behavior also change, then we would consider we had been successful. We have precisely done that. We studied for two years, we shared with each other, walked with each other, cried with each other and celebrated with each other and we are one in the kingdom of God. We have watched men and women from all races come to know Jesus as Lord and Savior and we continue this work. We decided that this will be our life-long work and it will not stop after the thesis-project is complete. We can say that we met every goal, listened to every concern, facilitated issues that came from a growing pains perspective and have found that whites and blacks are now praying together and Hispanics are feeling the love that comes from the body of Christ. Wonderful new relationships have formed and now we seek to serve the lost and provide a Christian base for men and women who are looking to have and live an inclusive lifestyle. We have been successful, and every person who started this journey is still in leadership. Furthermore we have taken in almost twenty families and our church has doubled from 80 to more than 160. To God be the Glory!

KEY LEARNINGS AS PASTOR

I learned that this process was a Herculean task and that it was much more difficult than I could ever have imagined. This task was changing me in every area of my life. I knew that I loved people and I knew that I loved God, but I learned to love at a deeper level. That has meant more to me than a project. I learned that white people like fried chicken and black people like beans and rice. I learned from my white family that hummus and celery is a very healthy snack. I learned that I have leadership skills that I had not realized before. I learned how to develop Sticky Teams and how to have Fierce Conversations and I learned that I may not have all the answers about racial divisions. I also learned that I am a redemptive leader who has created other redemptive leaders. I further learned that transformation is very real, and that people can be transformed and then do so much more. What God has done has been nothing short of a miracle. Lastly, I learned a valuable lesson that has caused me to lose some friends, i.e., that not everyone is ready to have the conversation or believes that the church should be inclusive. I am no longer invited to preach at many of my black pastor friends' churches because I they think that I am on a different team now. I have learned that when you are a pastor of a traditional black church and seek to move into a multi-ethnic context, people will try to make you think that you did not hear from God. I have learned that standing for God will sometimes mean that you will stand by yourself. Of all the lessons that I had to learn, that was the one that hurt the most. I now understand what Bishop I. Van Hilliard meant when he said,

"A LESSON NOT LEARNED FROM, SHALL BE REPEATED."[72]

I learned the lesson in hope that I will never have to feel that pain again.

The project that has been assigned to me is to be faithful to God and to walk according to his purposes for my life, and to fulfill the will of God that is recorded in the Great Commission. I am happy with the work that has been done; however, I wish that there was more research on this specific topic of transitioning an African American church plant and making it a multi-ethnic church. I would suggest that others who have done this type of work or who are African American and have successfully transitioned a church share their research. I hope that other students

72 Bishop Ira Van Hilliard, New Light Church, Houston, Texas.

who are African American will share their stories or even pick up where I leave off, sharing the good and the bad aspects of transitioning a church. Further research could possibly be conducted to show how to get people to respond to the call to multi-ethnic churches, how to develop cross cultural leadership, and how to gain the trust of people across races in a very race-driven society. We should also explore how to regain trust in people that are different, when the past dictates that you cannot do so.

I was fortunate that I did not have any causalities. I only had some personal disappointments. However, every person who started this journey with me has grown. They all serve as redemptive leaders and can testify that the redemptive model works. The community that I serve, along with some of the greatest people on this side of heaven, are all the better because we attempted to do what has not been done before at this level in Edgewood, Maryland. I want to encourage every person who is looking to conquer the odds to go for it. Stop worrying about failing. The great thing about failing is it gives you lessons that will ensure success is preeminent. God never told us that the work for which he called us would be easy. However, He did tell us that every step of the way he would be there to help us, motivate us, strengthen us, encourage us and push us. That's the God that we know and serve, the one who is able to keep us from falling. The one who creates a way of escape for us, so that we can bear every situation. You can do it! You can Conquer all. The only difference between you and me is that one day I grew tired of people telling me what I could be, when they did not make me. The crazy thing is, I had started believing that I was nothing. I had started for a brief minute believing that maybe, just maybe, I wasn't cut out for success. Do not believe anyone who tries to tell you that you cannot succeed! They do not know what they are talking about. You have everything that you need to be successful. Decide today that you are a conqueror and keep saying to yourself, "I Conquer!" If you need some reassurance when you wake up tomorrow, read this section of the book again. Trust the word of God in Philippians 1:6, where Paul ministers to the people and says, "He who has begun a good work in you shall perform it until the day of Jesus Christ." Today is your day, so give God a chance to show you that your best days are ahead of you and your worst days are behind you! I conquer and I am a conqueror and I will control my own destiny. So what are you waiting for?

GO CONQUER!

APPENDIX

RESEARCH QUESTIONNAIRE

This questionnaire is designed to gather information about your thoughts on transiting More Than Conquerors Worship Center into a Multi-Ethnic Church. This is an anonymous and confidential survey and at no time will you be asked to identify yourself. The information that you provide will be presented only in summary form, in combination with responses from other

participants. This questionnaire should take you about 10 minutes to complete. Thank you for taking the time to participate in this important project. By completing this anonymous questionnaire, you have given your consent that you are a voluntary participant in this study.

1. What is your age group:
   - o 15-25
   - o 25-35
   - o 35-45
   - o 45-55
   - o Over 55
2. Are you:
   - o Male
   - o Female
3. Do you believe in and support community worship? (The type of worship where everyone is welcome)

4. Would you be willing to assist someone from another race/culture feel comfortable at our church? (Please explain your response)

5. Would you be willing to go outside of the walls of the church to do intentional evangelism in the White, Hispanic, and Asian communities surrounding our church?

6. Would you welcome and support cultural diversity in our church?

7. Would you be open to having White, Asian and Hispanic persons join our church?? (Please explain your response)

8. If we were to have small group bible study and you were assigned to a group where the leader was from a different cultural group, would you:

   a. Still participate
   b. Be comfortable participating
   c. Feel comfortable sharing your heart in that setting

4. What do you feel was the theme of Matthew 6:10? The main purpose?

5. Would you support MTC being very intentional about welcoming, Black, White, Asian, Hispanic and Native Americans to worship with us.

6. Would you support having a diverse staff, leadership and or worship leader?

7. Would you just like for everything to stay the same?

8. Do you know how much your Pastor loves YOU???

Thank you for helping me with my research. Please forward all responses to Minister Michael Dykes *@Michael.a.dykes@gmail.com*. He will formulate the responses and send me the data.

BIBLIOGRAPHY

Anderson, David A. *Multicultural Ministry: Finding Your Church's Unique Rhythm.* Grand Rapids, MI: Zondervan, 2004.

Anderson, David A. and Brent Zuercher. *Letters Across the Divide: Two Friends Explore Racism, Friendship, and Faith.* Grand Rapids, MI: Bakers Books, 2001.

Blomberg, Craig L. *Matthew. The New American Commentary.* Nashville, TN: Broadman Press, 1992.

Bruner, Frederick D. *Matthew. A Commentary: The Christbook.* Grand Rapids, MI:Eerdmans, 2004.

Caffin, B.C. *Matthew.* The Pulpit Commentary. Peabody, MA: Hendrickson Publishers.

Chand, Samuel R. *Cracking Your Church's Culture Code: Seven Keys to Unleashing Vision and Inspiration.* San Francisco, CA: Jossey-Bass, 2011.

Clinton, J. Robert. *The Making of a Leader: Recognizing the Lessons and Stages of Leadership Development*. Colorado Springs, CO: NavPress, 1988.

Covey, Stephen. *The Seven Habits of Highly Effective People.* NY: Free Press, 1989.

DeYmaz, John M. *Building a Healthy Multi-ethnic Church: Mandate, Commitments, and Practices of a Diverse Congregation.* San Francisco, CA: Jossey-Bass/ Leadership Network, 2007.

DeYmaz, John M., and Harry W. Li. *Ethnic Blends: Mixing Diversity Into Your Local Church.* Grand Rapids, MI: Zondervan/Leadership Network, 2010.

DeYoung, Curtiss Paul; Michael O. Emerson, George Yancey, and Karen Chai Kim. *United By Faith: The Multiracial Congregation as an Answer to the Problem of Race*. New York: Oxford University Press, 2003.

Emerson, Michael O., Christian Smith. *Divided By Faith. Evangelical Religion and the Problem of Race in America.* New York: Oxford University Press, 2001.

R.T. France, *The Gospel of Matthew*. Grand Rapids, MI: Eerdmans, 2007.

Gilbreath, Edward. *Reconciliation Blues: A Black Evangelical's Inside View of White Christianity.* Downers Grove, IL: InterVarsity Press, 2006.

Guzick, David. "Study Guide for Matthew 6." *Blue Letter Bible*. https://www.blueletterbible.org/Comm/archives/guzik_david/studyguide_mat/mat_6.cfm

Heifetz, Ronald A., and Marty Linsky, *Leadership On The Line: Staying Alive through the Dangers of Leading*. Boston, MA: Harvard Business Review Press, 2002.

Henry, Matthew. "Commentary on Isaiah 56." *Blue Letter Bible*. https://www.blueletterbible.org/ Comm/mhc/Isa/Isa_056.cfm?a=735007

Keener, Craig S. *Matthew*. The IVP New Testament Commentary Series. Downers Grove, IL: InterVarsity, 1997.

A Commentary on the Gospel Of Matthew. Grand Rapids, MI: Eerdmans, 1999.

Ladd, George E. *A Theology Of The New Testament*. Grand Rapids, MI: Eerdmans, 1974.

Lingenfelter, Sherwood G. *Leading Cross-Culturally: Covenant Relationships for Effective Christian Leadership*. Grand Rapids, MI: Baker Academic, 2008.

Massey, Floyd, Jr and Samuel Berry McKinney. *Church Administration in the Black Perspective*. Valley Forge, PA: Judson Press, 1976.

Metger, Paul Louis. *Consuming Jesus: Beyond Race and Class Divisions in a Consumer Church*. Grand Rapids, MI: Wm. B. Eerdmans, 2008.

Olson, David T. *The American Church in Crisis: Groundbreaking Research on a National Data Base of Over 200,000 Churches.* Grand Rapids, MI: Zondervan, 2008.

Osborne, Larry. *Sticky Teams*. Grand Rapids, MI: Zondervan Publishers, 2010.

Oswalt, John N. *The Book of Isaiah*. Grand Rapids, MI :Eerdmanns.

Rah, Soong-Chan. *The Next Evangelicalism: Freeing the Church From Western Cultural Captivity*. Downers Grove, IL: InterVarsity Press, 2009.

Rah, Soong-Chan. *Many Colors: Cultural Intelligence for a Changing Church*. Chicago, IL: Moody Publishers, 2010.

Rawlinson G. *Isaiah*. Vol. 10 of *The Pulpit Commentary*. Peabody, MA: Hendrickson Publishers.

Reddish, Mitchell G. "Revelation." *Smyth & Helwys Bible Commentary*. Macon, GA: Smyth and Helwys, 2001.

Sampley, J. Paul. *2 Corinthians, Galatians, Ephesians, Philippians, Colossians, 1 & 2 Thessalonians, 1 & 2 Timothy, Titus, Philemon.* Vol. 11 of *The New Interpreter's Bible*. Nashville TN: Abingdon Press, 2000.

Schein, Edgar H. *Organizational Culture and Leadership*. San Francisco, CA: Jossey-Bass, 2010.

Smith, Christian, and Michael O. Emerson. *Divided by Faith: Evangelical Religion and the Problem of Race in America.* Oxford University Press, 2001.

Snyder, Howard A. *The Community of the King*. Downers Grove, IL: Inter Varsity Press, 2004.

Southerland, Dan. *Transitioning: Leading your Church Through Change*. Grand Rapids, MI: Zondervan, 1999.

Wiseman, Elizabeth with Greg McKeown. *Multipliers: How The Best Leaders Make Everyone Smarter*. New York: HarperCollins Publishers, 2010.

Woo, Rodney M. *The Color of Church: A Biblical and Practical Paradigm for Multiracial Churches.* Nashville, TN: B & H Academic, 2009.

Warren, Rick. *The Purpose Driven Church: Growth Without Compromising Your Message and Mission*. Grand Rapids, MI: Zondervan Publishers, 1995.

Yancey, George. *One Body, One Spirit: Principles of Successful Multiracial Churches.* Downers Grove, IL: InterVarsity Press, 2003.

Young, Edwin B. *The Creative Leader: Unleashing the Power of Your Creative Potential.* Nashville, TN: Broadman & Holman Publishers, 2006.

VITA

DERREN A. THOMPSON, SR.

Dr. Derren A. Thompson, Sr is a native of Baltimore where he joyfully serves as Pastor and visionary of The Conquerors Church in Edgewood, Maryland. This ministry is a multi-ethnic Bible-based fellowship of believers making a difference for the Kingdom of God.

Dr. Thompson is the CEO of Derren Thompson Ministries. This ministry is designed to minister to those who for whatever reason has been forgotten about and/or left behind. He has traveled across the country and on the islands of the Caribbean preaching and teaching the Good News of Jesus Christ. He owns with his wife Gone Again Travel Agency and has helped people across the country enjoy rest and relaxation.

He graduated with Honors from the University of Maryland Eastern Shore, with a B.S. Degree in Hotel Restaurant Management, and in May 2004, the Master of Divinity Degree was conferred upon him by the Samuel DeWitt Proctor School of Theology, Virginia Union University, Richmond, Virginia and in May 2018, he earned the Doctor of Ministry degree from Gordon Conwell Theological Seminary, Charlotte, NC in Redemptive Leadership.

Finally, Dr. Thompson is married to the former Chalon Melton of Los Angeles, California, and they are the proud parents of two sons, Derren, Jr. and Darius Alexander. In his spare time, he enjoys traveling the world which pushed him to start his own travel agency called Gone Again Travel. Dr. Thompson also enjoys serving as an Adjunct Professor at Morgan State University and his newest assignment teaching Human Resources Management at Cheyney University of Pennsylvania. He lives by the slogan and truth, that Jesus is the best thing that ever happened to him.

CPSIA information can be obtained
at www.ICGtesting.com
Printed in the USA
BVHW082047041021
618074BV00002B/10